CHINESE SNUFF BOTTLES

NO. 1. KU YUEH HSUAN. This is of painted milk glass, though they are sometimes of porcelain. It is the rarest, most exquisite, and most sought for of all snuff bottles. Shown here are the two sides and base of one with an exciting story behind it. From the collection of Albert Pyke, Los Angeles. See pages 93–94.

CHINESE SNUFF BOTTLES
The Adventures & Studies of a Collector

by LILLA S. PERRY

CHARLES E. TUTTLE COMPANY: PUBLISHERS
Rutland, Vermont & Tokyo, Japan

Dedicated to

GERTRUDE STUART

who introduced to me many of my collector
friends and brought to me from the
Orient my loveliest snuff bottles

REPRESENTATIVES

FOR CONTINENTAL EUROPE:
BOXERBOOKS, INC., ZURICH

FOR THE BRITISH ISLES:
PRENTICE-HALL INTERNATIONAL, INC., LONDON

FOR AUSTRALASIA:
PAUL FLESCH & CO., PTY. LTD., MELBOURNE

FOR CANADA:
M. G. HURTIG LTD., EDMONTON

PUBLISHED BY THE CHARLES E. TUTTLE COMPANY, INC
OF RUTLAND, VERMONT AND TOKYO, JAPAN
WITH EDITORIAL OFFICES AT
SUIDO 1-CHOME, 2–6, BUNKYO-KU, TOKYO, JAPAN

COPYRIGHT IN JAPAN, 1960
BY CHARLES E. TUTTLE CO., INC.
ALL RIGHTS RESERVED

LIBRARY OF CONGRESS CATALOG
CARD NO. 60–12196

STANDARD BOOK NO. 8048 0106-1

FIRST PRINTING, 1960
EIGHTH PRINTING, 1969

BOOK DESIGN AND TYPOGRAPHY BY K. OGIMI
LAYOUT OF ILLUSTRATIONS BY M. KUWATA

PRINTED IN JAPAN

TABLE OF CONTENTS

LIST OF ILLUSTRATIONS

Unless otherwise credited in the accompanying captions
all the snuff bottles illustrated are from the collection of
the author. An asterisk indicates a color plate.

ACKNOWLEDGMENTS

One does not write a book like this alone. I owe a debt of gratitude to the staff of the Gemological Institute of America for carefully going over the chapters on the stone bottles. Carl Sandburg read slowly through the first two chapters, pencil in hand, annihilating adjectives, dealing ruthlessly with adverbs. John Pope, of the Freer Galleries in Washington and an authority on porcelain, read and discussed with me the chapters on porcelain and the Ku Yueh Hsuan. One could hardly write about hornbill ivory and the inside-painted bottles without reference to the definitive research of Dr. Schuyler Cammann, of the University of Pennsylvania. P. T. Furst, of Los Angeles, linked his hobby to mine in enthusiastic photography of my collection of snuff bottles. Robert Moses, of Santa Barbara, painstakingly went through my manuscript for possible errors. My collector friends have cheered me on and have generously loaned me their treasures for illustrating my book. To all of these I owe a deep debt of gratitude.

LILLA S. PERRY

CHINESE SNUFF BOTTLES

CHAPTER ONE

On Collecting in General

Does anyone have as much fun as the enthusiastic collector? I doubt it. There is nothing that brings back the ecstatic emotion of being in love as does the glow that pervades the middle-aged collector in acquiring a new treasure. I know this, for I have felt it.

Collecting for most of us begins with our middle years. When young we are too eagerly collecting experiences of life to give our attention to objects of art. Lamenting to a fellow collector that our children seldom show interest in our collections I found his reply consoling. "They are too young. Do you know any collectors under forty or fifty?" I didn't, though they do exist, of course.

Collectors are either born or made. I was one of the "born." As a child of five I had a paste-board box that every night went under my bed holding my favorite toys. I can still see among them a tin horse with most of its paint worn off. Maybe this was my first collection, though my husband once said he was sure I must have secreted safety pins in my cradle.

Next came books, and in high school days I kept together all I had read and loved. There was Barrie's *Sentimental Tommy,* Olive Shreiner's *Story of an African Farm,* and many others that "I just couldn't live without." The trouble came when I went off to college and found that books are a problem to carry around. Later I collected quotations from books. My notebooks became many. This collection I have continued to this day. It garners the best of a library into small compass.

College days, marriage, collecting a family put a crimp into every other kind of collecting. A collection of Japanese prints and of Japanese *netsuke* limped along. Yet awareness and desire work wonders in building up a collection of anything.

Many years ago, visiting an old Indian who had an amazing assortment of arrowheads, of sizes to kill anything from a bird to a buffalo, I asked how he found them. His answer was, "You like something, you take good care of it, you think much about it, pretty soon others just like it—*they come!*"

Piece by piece a collection is built up. Slowness has its advantage. You find what books have to say. You investigate in museums and private collections. This can save you from mistakes.

Much is said today about what we are going to do with our leisure in this world of decreasing hours of labor, the years of retirement after a certain age. For a collector there need be no worry. Of course if his collection should be match covers or cigar bands I am not so sure. But if his pursuit is something the museums have considered worthy to house, he is safe. There is endless research to be done if he has chosen wisely.

Collecting brings friends. We share our interests. Even the person of limited budget may get into his car and cover a continent, and he will find the doors of similar collectors open to him everywhere.

Travel has an added zest for the collector, it has far greater zip for him than it does for the average tourist. There is a definite object in visiting museums, in seeking out shops which may yield treasures, and in finding other collectors. Is there a bored moment in travel? Not for him, though we may often feel sympathy for his fellow traveler.

That poor fellow traveler is often an uninterested mate. My own husband had interests similar to my own, but his enthusiasms were inhibited in his last days by the years of the depression and the stress period of bringing up a family. I laugh when I remember an afternoon spent in going through a pile of Japanese prints with him in the well-known Bentz Shop in Pasadena. There were two sheets of an Eisho triptych that seemed to us the most beautiful prints we had ever seen. As print collectors know, each single sheet of a triptych is often a complete composition in itself, as integrated in design as a separate movement of a sonata or a symphony. Each of these sheets contained figures of three women. One, we both agreed, in the arrangement of the design, was slightly superior to the other. In fact its perfection haunted me. Although by tacit consent I was sworn to economy in collecting I drove to Pasadena the following day and bought the print. I didn't intend to reveal my purchase immediately. I suppose I planned eventually to slip it among our other prints, and if it later evoked surprise or comment get off the time-worn remark, "Why, we've had that for a long time!"

Imagine my consternation when my husband remarked on the very next morning, "You know, I've kept thinking of that sheet of the Eisho triptych we liked so much. I believe the library's collection of prints should have it." (He was director of the public library of Los Angeles at the time.) "Drive over to Pasadena today, will you, and buy it for the library." I saw plainly that his loyalty to the library's collection was greater than to our own. But give up my precious treasure, how could I? The errand was delayed a few days to let his memory of the very similar prints blur a bit. Then I went over and bought the other sheet for the library, and there it is to this day. Nobody but another collector would understand such chicanery.

On another occasion the estate of a missionary to Japan was to be auctioned off in Long Beach, a collection of Japanese prints among them. This elderly man had passed his life in Japan during the heyday of print buying, when Kiyonagas and Utamaros could easily have come his way. My mother, who followed me in all my enthusiasms, joined me in attending the auction. There we met an old friend, Mr. Judson D. Metzgar, well known as an expert on Japanese prints.

Our preview was disappointing. The collection was to be sold as a lot and there was none of the work of the greatest print artists in it. If it went cheaply enough, however, there was much to interest us. The collection consisted mainly of triptychs mounted with wide margins on large slabs of Bristol board. They were not really a negligible group. We glimpsed among them a number of fine prints by Kiyochika, a late man, but good.

Mr. Metzgar and I decided that between us we would give fifty dollars for them and divide them later. This may appear a very low bid, but remember these were depression days. I was to do the bidding since I was an unknown and Mr. Metzgar was well known as a print expert to the number of dealers there. The bidding stopped at fifty dollars, and the prints were ours.

Those large slabs of Bristol board! They wouldn't go on the back seat of my car. We put little Mother there and piled them in around her. They stuck out of the windows like planks of lumber. We dropped Mr. Metzgar off at his hotel with the prospect of an exciting day on the morrow dividing up our purchase. "I'm glad we are getting home early," I declared to Mother. "I'll have a chance to get this 'lumber' out of the car and stowed away before the man of the house appears."

It was fated to be otherwise, however. As I turned into our driveway I beheld my husband, home at an unusually early hour, just putting his own car into the garage. Our respective cars had long been named Pomp and Circumstance. Circumstance had no garage space. Being the humbler of the two cars it was parked between the latticed sides of a more or less unused tea garden. Realizing how my burdened car must look and in no way wanting to account at the moment for all those prints, I was so upset that I drove straight through the end lattice of my parking space. Down it came with a bang!

"For Heaven's sake, is that the way you park your car!"

"Not usually," I answered feebly. "You startled me, kind sir! Aren't you home a bit early?"

"What if I am? You'll have to get a carpenter tomorrow to fix up that damage." He took my arm and walked me into the house, solicitously, as though he feared me slightly deranged. The crash had created a diversion. He had noticed neither my "lumber" nor little Mother behind it all in the back seat.

Of course, now I relish the collecting experiences of others. I was amused when I came upon the following passage in reading Carl Sandburg's book on the great Lincolniana collection of Oliver R. Barrett:

"For some years after his marriage Barrett had a system when bringing home an armload of books and manuscripts. He laid them gently and quietly outside the front basement window. Later at night he would go to the basement and, as casually as you please, bring his new acquisitions upstairs as if from his old basement stock. This smuggling system came to an end when a law partner, in retaliation for a practical joke, repaid in kind and told how the system worked—and it ended. The collector was forced to devise new methods."

Edward Newton, in *The Amenities of Book Collecting* says, "When I am going to be extravagant I always like the encouragement of my wife, and I usually get it. I determined to talk over with her a proposed purchase. Her prophetic instinct in this instance was against it. Her advice was good, indeed, her arguments were so unanswerable that I determined not to discuss it further, but to buy it anyway and say nothing."

A collector of antiques has just told me this story: Her husband had at last complained that enough was enough. A truce was agreed upon that for a while there should be no further buying of antiques. One day, however, she came upon a petit-point footstool that was irresistible. She had to have it. It would escape notice. But just as she was coming from her garage into her kitchen with the footstool in her hand she heard her husband's footsteps approaching. The deep-freeze stood near. She opened the cover and thrust it in. It was the maid's day out and later when they began to talk about dinner, "Let's have a couple of those thick steaks that are in the deep-freeze," her husband exclaimed. "No, don't move. I'll get them out," he added chivalrously. There was no stopping him, and a few minutes later she had to face him as he stood in the doorway holding up the petit-point stool by one leg. "Since when do we keep such things in deep-freeze?"

It is not always the men who are the protesters. One of my pet collector stories is about a man whose friend turned to him and said, "What's the matter with you today, Jim? I've never seen you when you acted so depressed."

"Well, I *am* depressed," replied Jim. "Last night my wife said to me, 'If you bring another of those darned things into the house I'm going to leave you!' And, by Jove, I'm going to miss her!"

Need I add to the list of perquisites and declare that there is humor in collecting? I can contend, too, that for the true collector there is always drama and adventure, and you will come upon plenty in the chapters that follow.

CHAPTER TWO

On Collecting Snuff Bottles in Particular

Collecting has somewhat the thrill of being caught up in some alluring, inescapable love affair. The object of our enthusiasm more often chooses us than we do the choosing. A man's doctor will sometimes say to him, "You are too concentrated on your business. You need a good hobby to slow you down." Such a man is completely lost as he begins to look around. He may half-heartedly take on some project that soon peters out. There is as little kick to it as in the case of the man who quite deliberately and without any one person in mind, decides that he ought to get married. Don't collect unless you find yourself driven by a deep enthusiasm.

Try to collect things which do not take up too much room. In the apartments and the small houses in which the present generation lives that is desirable. If your partner seems unlikely to share your project it will of a certainty annoy him less if your collection takes little space. You may now convict me of pulling for Chinese snuff bottles as ideal objects to collect. Perhaps I am. I am remembering that a small cabinet, projecting not more than three inches from a wall, may easily hold all the Chinese snuff bottles that one would ever want.

Suppose you collect antique furniture. In doing so you may be creating an entire environment for your unenthusiastic partner. If he complains that the chairs are not comfortable, that the treasured secretary desk has seventeen cubbies and drawers (unlabelled, of course) and to find anything he has to rummage through them all, you may with good reason develop a guilty conscience. You are requiring him to live surrounded by the utilities and the accoutrements of a long departed generation. If he explodes, "Why do we have to live in a period setting not our own? Why must we live in this museum?" you may feel him quite justified.

Be grateful yourself if your partner has not early begun the accumulating of firearms and armor. He will have you crowded into a corner or keep you forever looking for a larger home.

The advantage of a collection that can be compressed into small space is surely not to be overlooked. There is nothing oppressive about a collection of small bottles which can be put completely out of sight in five minutes. Be sure you possess your collection. Do not let it possess you. For collecting is not the whole of life. It is one of its delightful diversions. There are times when it needs to be dropped entirely out of sight.

A second suggestion: try to let your choice be something that the museums of the country have considered worthy to house. There is hardly a large museum in the United States that does not contain its collection of Chinese snuff bottles. Whether they have them on display or will get them out of storage for your inspection is another story. They are recognized as works of art, however, and as such will have been conserved.

As a girl I visited a relative and came upon this situation. The wife had asked her husband to pick up a common cream pitcher to replace one that she had broken. The first one he bought was a dripper. Women will know what I mean. So he set forth once more to find a cream pitcher. By this time he had become interested in cream pitchers, so he brought home two. He had by now become cream-pitcher conscious. He couldn't pass a display of china without looking for a better

NO. 2: LAPIS LAZULI. At its best a sparkling blue, though we often find it as dull as a woman's blue serge dress. Wait for one with the right color. What we want has a way of coming to us. See page 108.

NO. 3. MALACHITE. Often found carved, its softness making it appealing to the lapidary. Many collectors, however, prefer to let the beauty of the uncarved stone speak for itself. See page 108.

NO. 4. TOURMALINE. A translucent stone ranging from pale pink to deep rose. Green and yellow tourmaline also exist, however. They give collectors something to search for. See page 107.

NO. 5. FLUORITE. Easily mistaken for aquamarine, its color so similar. Soft enough to be the delight of the lapidary, but not often used because of its fragility. See page 107.

NO. 6. AQUAMARINE. Sea blue in color. Though this bottle shows exquisite carving, I prefer an uncarved bottle where depth and purity of color alone speak. See pages 110–11.

one, or a different one, or an odd and unusual shaped one. And the pitchers kept coming home! My aunt, as I called her, was driven crazy by them. She showed me her closets, everything crowded out to make room for the cream pitchers. It had become a feud between them, and why wouldn't it? "How I wish I had never asked him to buy me that cream pitcher!" she moaned. I never knew how it ended. Uncle died soon after, and I never heard what became of the pitchers. Scattered as gifts, probably. What else was there to do with them?

Once calling upon an acquaintance whose wealth would have enabled her to collect diamonds and rubies had she so chosen, I wandered down her huge drawing room to inspect the contents of two corner cupboards. They seemed to contain *little* things. *Netsuke*, I thought, or perhaps even Chinese snuff bottles! They did contain little things, tiny porcelain cats and rabbits and dogs, all kinds of animals, in fact. And in addition there were innumerable miniatures of furniture. You might think you were viewing in dismantled array the contents of those miniature rooms of period furniture which Mrs. James Ward Thorne so cleverly assembled. Some of you will remember that they were exhibited at many of the great fairs and are now permanently housed at the Chicago Art Institute. Mrs. Thorne's display was fascinating. There was reason and meaning in it.

It showed us the typical drawing room of many periods. We observed change and development. But here! This unrelated collection of objects! It led nowhere, certainly into no research of any kind. It touched the history of art or craftsmanship at no point. I turned away disturbed. I mention this, because I believe *what* we collect is important. There must be mental stimulus in it.

There is plenty of challenge to research in collecting Chinese snuff bottles. So little is known about them, so little has been written about them. To date, though I have heard about books in progress, there is only one book in any language that has ever appeared. It is a handmade, lithographed book, put together by an American, Mr. Henry C. Hitt, in 1945. It has long been out of print. He called it, *Old Chinese Snuff Bottles: Notes, with a Catalogue of a Modest Collection.*

At the time I visited him at his home in Bremerton, Washington, he expressed his amazement that the book had attracted so much attention. Museums, librarians, and private collectors all over the country had sent for it. He could hardly keep up with the orders. He modestly laid it to the complete dearth of material on the subject. He was right. He admitted the book was exploratory on his theme. In it he called for correspondence and corrections. He got plenty of both. It was not too good a book. His collection of bottles contained few that were notable. Of course pictures of them in color would have been far more telling than his laborious drawings and black-and-white photographs.

At the time he wrote the book he had not yet made his journey over the country seeing other collections. He freely admitted many mistakes he had made on which his many correspondents had set him straight. He was completely in error in almost everything he had to say about the inside-painted bottles. Schuyler Cammann has since that time done fine research on that subject. His work has settled the moot points and is probably definitive. Mr. Hitt, however, was a good pioneer. His book had tremendous value in that it stirred up the collectors everywhere, even in China.

In 1946 when I was in Washington, D.C., I questioned the curator of Oriental books in the Library of Congress about the literature on snuff bottles in Chinese. He knew of no book that had ever been written, he said, and a short investigation by him indicated that there had been none. Yet against the walls in his department there stood in microfilm every book and manuscript of the great Peking Library. Our government had been asked to take the responsibility of storing it at the time of the Chinese-Japanese trouble, and we agreed to do so if we were permitted to duplicate the library for ourselves in microfilm.

"There are paragraphs and perhaps a few pages about the snuff bottles in books which deal with the materials of which the bottles are made," the curator commented. "The bottles would probably be mentioned in books on porcelain, on glassmaking, on ivory carving, and other places. There exists no separate book about them, however."

Quite recently I have learned that there is a book in Chinese about the snuff bottles. How recently it was written I do not know, but I saw a translation of it at the home of Gerry Mack, a New York collector. It ran to only thirty or thirty-five type-written pages as I remember, however, so it can hardly be considered more than a brochure. Perhaps it is the same manuscript of which Schuyler Cammann promises the publication of a translation shortly. Collectors will want to watch for this.

Every year that I have gone East from my home in California I have visited an old friend of mine. He was a college classmate, whose wife, strangely enough, for it doesn't often happen, I have come to enjoy as much as himself. Because of the certainty of shared interests I have almost every time taken with me a few examples of some one of my collections.

On my last visit I had with me one of those sectioned-off, satin-padded boxes which hold ten Chinese snuff bottles. Most of them were of semiprecious stones. The rose of the tourmaline, the transparent blue of the aquamarine, the gold-flecked lapis lazuli, the green swirls of the malachite, the soft pink of the tenderly carved coral set each other off with a fanfare of color that none could quite have given off alone (Nos. 2–6).

My hosts were delighted with them. My friend is an engineer, scientific-minded but with a probing interest in many other fields. He has been an inveterate hiker, and a ten-mile walk has always meant more to him that the mere physical motion it would mean to me. He takes in the terrain like a geologist and a botanist. Rocks and plants of many kinds are on naming-acquaintance. He is likely to appear home at last with a handful of diamond-point arrowheads in his pocket or with some strange artifact that his toe has kicked up in a newly ploughed field.

"Let me see if I can name the material of these things," he exclaimed as he looked at my bottles. He could, all except one delicately carved blue bottle that a collector would swear was aquamarine (No. 5). It had taken a testing at the Gemological Institute of America to determine that it was fluorite. This is an institute with headquarters in Los Angeles and branches in other large cities to which we collectors bring or send our bottles when their material is in dispute.

"This collection of Chinese snuff bottles is the most interesting thing you have brought us yet!" my friend commented. "Every year you have something different to show us. You have been consistent," he might have added, "in that they have always been in the realm of Oriental art. One year you brought a collection of sword guards and amazingly decorated dagger handles. It was easy to see how you could get interested in those. One year you had with you a portfolio of Japanese prints of an old vintage, *ukiyo-e,* you called them. You followed the next time with a collection of the work of contemporary Japanese woodblock artists. We didn't go for those as much, though your enthusiasm was certainly contagious. Last time, in a sectioned-off box like this, you had a sampling of your collection of Japanese *netsuke.* They were amazing things, really miniature masterpieces of sculpture. But these!—these Chinese snuff bottles, these are the most beautiful, the most interesting of all your collections."

This is the opinion that would be given by almost all non-collectors. The appeal of a beautiful Chinese snuff bottle is indeed immediate. Its intrinsic value is right before you. You need know nothing about it, nothing of its history, its utility, its material, or its origin. It is simply "a thing of beauty and a joy forever." For the non-collector isn't that enough?

Ellen Shaffer, in her excellent articles on snuff bottles in *Antiques Journal,* quotes Marcus Huish, "Little or no training is necessary to distinguish their genuineness or their merit. These lie on the surface, and are, for the most part, incapable of imitation." Then she adds her own comment, "In other words, if you have some knowledge—intuitive or otherwise—of fine workmanship in general, you will recognize it in a snuff bottle."

Now, suppose you are a generous person and that you graciously hand over one of your bottles as a gift to your non-collector. That may only mean that you have two or three more of the same type of bottle. When he expresses his surprise and pleasure you may add the bit of information that you know a certain shop where very fine bottles may be purchased at prices that are very reasonable. Then, indeed, is your non-collector lost and a new collector found.

Many Chinese snuff bottle collections that I know have begun in this way— with gifts. My own did. When you get that one lonely, lovely bottle home and set it on a shelf, you are struck with both adjectives I have used. It is, indeed, very lovely and it looks so tiny and alone. You begin to imagine a few others around it. "Five of anything," someone has said, "makes a collection." You are indeed hooked! The making of a collection begins.

CHAPTER THREE

The Story of the Bottles in China

The fashion of taking snuff started in both China and Europe almost at the same time, roughly about 1650. Accept this date of 1650 as very rough indeed. Personally, I have a terrible memory for dates and do better with round numbers. I use this date also because there seems to be so little agreement among the authorities as to its precise beginning. There are those who believe that the taking of snuff began as early as in the Ming dynasty which just preceded the Manchu. The consensus of opinion is against this, however, and we shall not be far from the truth if we think of the beginnings, the culmination, and the final discontinuance of snuff taking as coinciding very closely with the rise and fall of the Manchu dynasty, from 1644 until 1912, when the Chinese Republic was proclaimed and the Manchu dynasty was at an end.

Mattoon M. Curtis, in his *Book of Snuff and Snuff Boxes,* says, "Snuff played a considerable social role for about three hundred years in the life of all peoples. . . . Tobacco's first speedy conquest was the maritime world, then the great port cities, and finally the Church and the State capitals of the world. About 1575 it was used in every nation of the earth."

It is his belief that tobacco was introduced to China from Europe about 1537, basing this conviction, doubtless, on the fact that the Portuguese established the first European colony in the Far East at Macao on the fringe of China about that time. He goes on to say, " Soon after its introduction snuffing seems to have become the favorite form of its consumption. We might call the period from 1537 to 1644 one of adaptation of the bottle to the uses of snuff." He admits, however, that the great period of the snuff bottle is that of the Manchu dynasty 1644 to 1912.

Since the story of the snuff bottle roughly coincides with this dynasty, with varying fate during the reign of each emperor, let us have the dates of each of these reigns before us. They can be found in many of the books on Oriental art. They are often conveniently tabulated for us on the business cards of dealers in

Oriental wares. But when we want these dates they are not always immediately available. Let's have them here before us for ready reference as we tell our story.

REIGN PERIODS OF MANCHU DYNASTY EMPERORS

Shun Chih	(1644–1661)	Tao Kuang	(1821–1850)
K'ang Hsi	(1662–1722)	Hsien Fêng	(1851–1861)
Yung Chêng	(1723–1735)	T'ung Chih	(1862–1874)
Ch'ien Lung	(1736–1795)	Kuang Hsü	(1875–1908)
Chia Ch'ing	(1796–1820)	Regency	(1909–1912)

The story of the snuff bottle and its use in China strangely parallels the tale of the snuff box in Europe. The use of tobacco and of snuff, too, met violent opposition on both continents. Louis XIV (1643–1715), though he tiraded against the use of snuff in his court and issued edicts against it, was said to have been a user of it himself. Among the Manchus, too, it was frowned upon at first as a messy habit. Perhaps this was before the snuff bottle, as such, with its tight cork and tiny spoon for the removal of the powder, had been fully developed. At the beginning it is known that various containers were used, medicine and perfume bottles and many miniature vases of convenient size were converted to snuff-container use and may have proved none too adequate. Some of our snuff bottles today are recognizable miniature porcelain vases. The lip of the vase presents a rounded surface instead of the flat one of the real snuff bottle. The bottle top could never have fitted as closely. Curtis tells us that in Europe also earlier types of boxes were at first used for the snuff: bonbon and powder containers. "One knows the true snuff box," he admits, "more by intuition than by definition."

Though makeshifts were at first used for containers of the snuff it was not long before the artists and craftsmen of both continents were called into service to produce the most beautiful containers possible for this fragrant powder whose use had become the vogue in all the courts.

It is probably because the Oriental had no pocket and the container had to be carried in his sleeve that the Oriental used bottles while the European used boxes. R. L. Hobson, in the British Museum *Handbook of the Pottery and Porcelain of the Far East,* tells us that it is highly improbable that the orthodox porcelain snuff bottle with its spoon and stopper came into use before the eighteenth century. That would still give us twenty-two years left of K'ang Hsi's reign during which his patronage and encouragement brought about intense development of all the arts. The making of snuff bottles flourished through his and the two succeeding reigns. It is fairly certain that the pinnacle of their production was reached in the reigns of K'ang Hsi, Yung Chêng, and Ch'ien Lung.

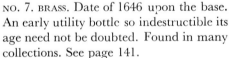

NO. 7. BRASS. Date of 1646 upon the base. An early utility bottle so indestructible its age need not be doubted. Found in many collections. See page 141.

NO. 8. MULTIPLE BRASS. Eight small attached bottles, equipped with their own spoon and stopper. A unique bottle. From the collection of Russell Mullin, Beverly Hills. See page 141.

NO. 9. IRON WITH SILVER INSET. Another unique bottle not likely to have been duplicated. Also from the collection of Russell Mullin. See page 142.

In this day when the moving-picture world has set a fashion of super-thinness for women I often see my middle-aged friends, afraid of a pound of overweight, take from their purses at a luncheon or dinner a tiny inch-square box containing saccharin and drop a pellet into their tea or coffee. The boxes are of various materials, some of them very beautiful. What an idea for a gift, one thinks, and stows it away in one's mind for some friend who seems to have everything. Will our great great grandchildren be collecting them one wonders.

Curtis tells us that the oldest dated snuff box known is an oval in silver, of 1655. The oldest bottle in my collection is dated 1646 (No. 7). It is marked on the base, Shun Chih, third year. Shun Chih's reign began in 1644. This would date the bottle 1646. It is a brass one, similar to the type described in Mr. Hitt's book on Chinese snuff bottles, now out of print. There are a number of them to be found in various collections. Such bottles are practically indestructible. There seems no reason to doubt their authenticity.

In spite of opposition in China as well as in Europe, it was not long before the use of snuff became a social ritual of the upper classes. When two Chinese friends met there was at once an exchange of snuff, some of it very costly we are told, and the containers upon which much art and taste and money had been expended became "conversation pieces" between the two.

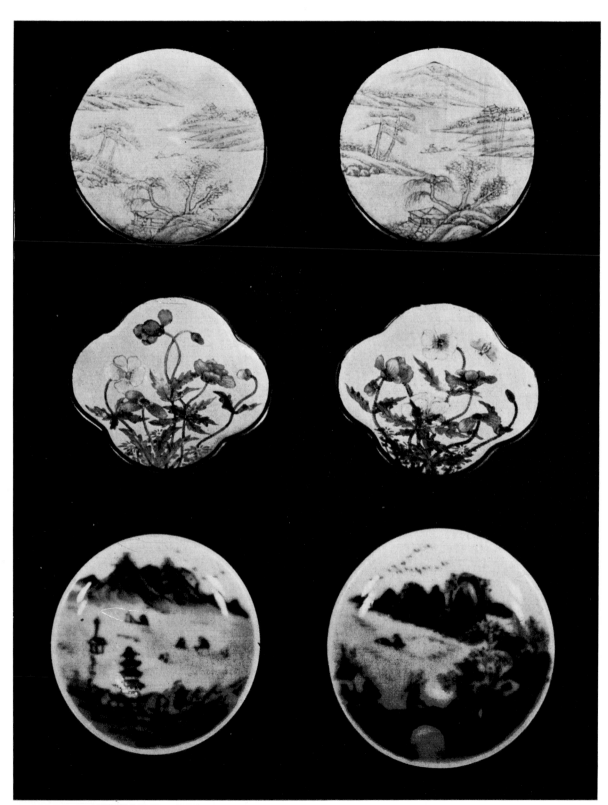

SNUFF SAUCERS. In the homes snuff was kept in large, table bottles. Snuff saucers like these, shown here a little larger than actual size, were distributed for use by guests. Top two rows, enamel on metal; bottom row, underglaze blue-and-white porcelain. From the collection of the Seattle Art Museum.

IVORY SCOOP AND FUNNEL. Ivory scoops and funnels like these were used to fill the bottles with snuff. Courtesy of Gertrude Stuart, Los Angeles.

The snuff taking seems to have been done daintily. Each snuff bottle was equipped with a tight stopper, a tiny spoon of ivory or silver or tortoise shell attached. The spoon, sometimes shaped as a tiny hand, was used to transfer a bit of snuff to the thumb-nail and from there was sniffed up by the aristocratic nose.

In the homes larger bottles, table bottles we call them now, were in evidence for the use of guests, as our cigarette containers are today. Small snuff saucers were distributed to guests also for the use of their snuff. These were made of as many materials as the bottles themselves and many people now collect them. An ivory scoop and funnel were used for getting the snuff into a bottle. The shaft of the scoop was used for tamping the snuff down.

It has ever been an Oriental trait to make of an object of use a thing of beauty. The use of the snuff bottle coincided with the time when great art development was taking place under the patronage of the three Manchu monarchs I have mentioned before. It is little wonder that there should have been lavished upon the snuff bottle all the upsurge of the art activity taking place throughout the realm.

The reign of Shun Chih, the first Manchu emperor, from 1644 to 1661, was doubtless one of adjustment. The Manchus had just taken over a disturbed country. But with the accession of K'ang Hsi in 1662 the country was under more control and in the hands of a wise ruler. He was, moreover, a devoted patron of the arts. He established during his reign twenty-seven imperial workshops in Peking, covering as many branches of art industry. Craftsmen were brought from all over the empire to produce in these studios their finest work. They were in existence for over a hundred years until the death of K'ang Hsi's grandson, Ch'ien Lung, another patron of the arts. The finest of the snuff bottles must surely have been made during this time.

There was hardly one of these workshops that could not have produced, as a work of art, the tiny snuff bottle. It has, as we collectors know, appeared in every conceivable material. I have not yet reached an end to the list of the various types that the collectors and museums have found.

AMBER: clear, opaque, and root amber. There is even a processed amber. There are also inside-painted amber bottles.

ENAMEL: in three forms, painted, cloisonné, champlevé.

GLASS: monochrome, plain or carved, painted or enameled, overlay or cameo type, imitations of many other materials.

HORN: rhinoceros, buffalo, and other horn carvings.

IVORY: carved and painted.

JADE: carved, uncarved, embellished, and in every color.

METALS: gold, silver, pewter, brass, bronze, iron.

POTTERY: carved, painted, enameled.

PORCELAIN: monochrome, carved decoration, applied decoration, pierced, underglaze decoration, enamel overglaze, incised, lacquered.

SEMIPRECIOUS STONES: tourmaline, aquamarine, green and other color beryl, malachite, turquoise, lapis lazuli, serpentine, fluorite, ruby.

QUARTZ: crystal, hair crystal, smoky crystal, amethyst quartz, rose quartz, chalcedony, agate, moss agate, jasper, carnelian, bloodstone, sardonyx, onyx, aventurine, cat's-eye.

MISCELLANEOUS: coral, lacquer, *laque burgauté,* mother-of-pearl, soapstone, woods of various kinds, nut, bamboo, dried tangerine skin, hornbill ivory, calcite, fossil stone, tortoise shell, jet, slate, inside-painted bottles of many materials, embellished bottles of many different basic materials.

All of these kinds I have seen in snuff bottles. I doubt if we can ever feel that our list is complete.

Throughout the reign of the early Manchu emperors the bottles must have been greatly in demand. Not only were they needed for the carrying of snuff, but the choice ones made the perfect gift. Never was there a time when the making of lavish gifts was a more prevalent custom. Furthermore, the emperors and many of the court nobles made collections of them. This, also, made them desirable gifts. There is a record that Ho Chen, chief advisor to Ch'ien Lung, had a collection of 2,390. In his position, as President of the Ministry of Civil Appointments, he must have received a stream of these gifts from the remotest provincial governors to the highest nobles at court. According to Eastern practice there was nothing dishonorable in his acceptance of presents. When he fell into disfavor with Ch'ien Lung's successor, Chia Ch'ing, the bottles were dug up from the spot where Ho Chen had buried them for safety and were confiscated.

This custom of gift making, except in Chia Ch'ing's penurious reign, must have continued to the present day. When the late Dr. Hanson's Oriental collection was sold on the Pacific coast his widow explained that on the payment of a bill for his medical services in China a present was always added, usually some work of art when his patients became aware of his art interest.

With more than a hundred years of imperial art patronage during the reigns of K'ang Hsi, Yung Chêng, and Ch'ien Lung, and with a flourishing demand for snuff bottles for use, for gifts, and for collections, these years were the heyday of snuff bottle production.

We get a vivid picture of the art activity of that period in one of the histories of China, *Hills of Blue* by A. E. Grantham.

"Dazzling magnificence at Court represented the crowning outburst, the topmost blossoming of the accumulated wealth of a whole people. The Imperial palaces were by no means the only ones in Peking. A crowd of rich families, nobles, merchants, ministers also built themselves sumptuous mansions decorated with exquisitely carved woodwork, furnished with heavy chests full of gorgeous silks and furs, with long lacquer tables displaying porcelains, jades and coral trees, with enormous cupboards stacked with books and picture-rolls, with couches inlaid with cloisonné.

"The monasteries, too, with their abundance of bronze images and incense bowls, brocade-bound manuscripts and jeweled shrines were vast repositories of treasure. Besides, public granaries and private warehouses were full to overflowing, shops and markets crowded with goods and customers. And this prosperity prevailed not only in the capital but in hundreds of cities nestling with well-built, well-kept temples, banks and shops around the bright tiled bell-tower and drumtower, within the grey ring of their walls.

"The population, estimated at 180 million in 1750, by 1795 almost reached 300 million, a remarkable increase.

"Probably at no time or place in the history of the world were craftsmen more active, more ingenious, more encouraged than in the China of Ch'ien Lung. Manipulating with equal dexterity every kind of material, metals, stone, pottery, wood, horn, leather, amber, lacquer, mother-of-pearl, the output of their myriads of looms, lathes, kilns and workshops was amazing in quantity, endless in variety, ranging from tiny egg-shell vases light and translucent as a bubble, to massive bronze lions and solid blocks of sculptured jade.

"So much skill, fantasy, and loving care had gone into the making of beautiful objects, the fashion to amass them became irresistible. Antiques, of course, had always been and continued to be assiduously collected. But now there were collectors of new things also. The abundance was so great that after 130 years of the most reckless wear and tear, the mere remnants still gladden an impoverished world with glimpses of the old enchantment."

It is not difficult to believe that the best of the bottles were produced during this period or to realize that, with the end of Ch'ien Lung's reign and the accession of his very different son, Chia Ch'ing, the making of the finest bottles began to come to an end.

Chia Ch'ing was no patron of the arts. What encouragement could there have been to continue to make bottles except in utility form under a monarch who declared that "decoration is merely a foolish squandering of funds"? Thrift and economies of all sorts were his constant aim, and he announced in one edict, "Things merely gratifying the eyes and the ears have no appeal to me whatever." In another edict about the kind of present he was willing to accept on one of his birthdays he warned would-be donors that if they presented anything made of pearls or jade he would not honor it with so much as a glance.

His disapproval of extravagance in gifts extended, of course, to the exchange of gifts among the members of a once generous and art-loving court. It was ridiculous that in a country where the production of beautiful silks and brocades was a leading industry he suddenly ordered the court to take up the wearing of cotton clothes. Fashions in vogue among the ladies of his court could upset his peace of mind. In the ninth year of his reign he made the horrifying discovery that women changed their styles. He laid down rules about this, but his only means of checking on their conduct was to make fathers and brothers responsible and liable to punishment should any case of disobedience come to light. Even the empress, when her allotted rolls of brocade had been stolen from the treasury where they were kept, was not allowed an extra supply. She had to make last year's dresses do! Is it any wonder that the art workshops languished or were discontinued? In the face of such imperial disapproval where would the fine artist or artisan have found a market for his product?

Very often when we collectors of today have been offered for our consideration a fine *laque burgauté* bottle or one of exquisitely painted milk glass, with the mark of Ch'ien Lung or Yung Chêng upon its base, I have heard scepticism expressed as to its dating as far back as these reigns. I have in my files the hilarious comments of one sceptical collector who voices the doubts of others as well:

"I have just done New York City, up and down and across, for three weeks. What a racket! The dealers and collectors dribble Ch'ien Lung and K'ang Hsi from their tongues like water over Niagara and know not whereof they speak, or don't want to know. Some of their bottles they actually believe to be three years older than God!"

Well, scepticism is all right, and it certainly behooves the collector to be cautious about paying a large price for a bottle which might be made with ease today, and in quantity. Where since the death of Ch'ien Lung, however, has there been incentive for the artist or craftsman to spend weeks upon a work of art? Certainly not in the twenty-four years of Chia Ch'ing's paralyzing effect upon art industry. Was there incentive in the export trade? Hardly. There was always a cheapening of the products that were produced for "the barbarian." The best work was always for the deeply appreciative Chinese connoisseur.

There may have been strays, of course, beautiful objects made for the sheer love of creating them. But it is the common story that when a market fails, production ceases. No artist lives and works in a vacuum. Large production of bottles of great beauty was most certainly at an end.

Following the crushing effect of Chia Ch'ing, where was there any restorative effect upon the arts in the reigns that followed, Tao Kuang's, Hsien Fêng's, T'ung Chih's, and Kuang Hsü's? The last three emperors, weak and decadent rulers, were under the domination of the Empress Dowager. They did nothing to revive the art of the earlier Manchu emperors. The biographers of the powerful Empress Dowager admit that though she was extravagant and luxury loving, she adorned her palaces with the treasures created in former days. She was no promoter of the art of her own time.

The histories of China have little to say of this later Manchu period except to describe the constant warfare, the invasions, and the internal rebellions in which the nation was plunged. Few speak of its effect on art production. Mary Nourse in *A Short History of the Chinese* does mention it, however. She quotes Abel Bernard as saying, "The arts had perished, only the handicrafts continued like branches on a fallen oak, which put forth green, without knowing that the tree is dead."

This then, in brief outline, is the story of the snuff bottle in China. From its beginning to the present day it covers roughly little more than three hundred years. The claim of three hundred years of age does not make an antique in the Oriental mind. To him it is quite modern, in fact. Even to the Occidental, accustomed to thinking in Oriental terms, there is no antiquity here. Ernest F. Fenollosa, in *Epochs of Chinese and Japanese Art,* entitles his fifteenth chapter, "Modern Chinese Art: The Manchu Dynasty."

Might it not be better for the collector of Chinese snuff bottles, in view of their comparative modernity, to forget age and base his judgments upon fine workmanship, fine material, and design?

Juliet Bredon in 1922 wrote a book about Peking. The last of the Manchus had been gone for a decade. China was now a republic. The purpose of her book, she says, is to take us by the arm for a stroll through the city. She draws us toward the Forbidden City, that city within a walled city, that mysterious winter palace of the emperors, itself surrounded by a wall and known to have been closed for centuries. Here we meet a startling innovation. The Halls of Audience of the Forbidden City have now been made into a museum. It is open to the public. We walk through this place of treasures with her. When she passes the glass cases which contain the most valuable porcelain we follow expectantly. Yes, we come, she tells us, upon a case of Chinese snuff bottles. What an exciting moment for the collector of these precious things! Here should be the most beautiful and rare snuff bottles in the world. Are they the collection of the great art-patron emperors? Of what materials are they made? Whose timeless genius went into their design and carving? But, alas, she moves on. She describes not one of them.

And today, in this time of the Communist regime, all of China has seemingly become once more for us a Forbidden City.

ments as he discussed my own few bottles and some boxes of his own bottles that he had brought with him.

"All these terms, nephrite, jadeite, quartz, carnelian, agate, chalcedony, etc. must be very confusing to you. At the risk of repeating some things that you know, let me try to straighten them out in your mind. Let's begin with jade. There are two stones that come under the name of jade, nephrite and jadeite. This bottle," he said, picking up one of mine, "is a spinach jade, as we describe it. It is nephrite. Notice its soft waxy lustre. On the other hand, this green jade," lifting one from his own collection," is jadeite. It has a much higher polish and a vitreous or glassy appearance. Among the green jades it has a more brilliant color than we find in nephrite."

There were a number of jade bottles before us, and he tested me in determining whether they were nephrite or jadeite. I did pretty well. With his descriptions and the examples before me it was a fine way to learn.

"Jewel or imperial jade, as they call it, is always jadeite," he went on. "But we won't ever find a real imperial jade in a snuff bottle. It is perhaps the most valuable of all the jades and if found would never be carved into a bottle. In the form of fine jewelry it would bring much more money. Sometimes when there is a question of what type of jade a bottle may be, you may have to get it tested for its specific gravity and its hardness. Nephrite has a specific gravity of 3.0, hardness 6.5. Jadeite has a specific gravity of about 3.3 and a hardness of 7.

"You asked me to test this white stone bottle of yours. I found it had a specific gravity of 2.64, so it couldn't be jade. It is white quartz. By the way, if you aren't familiar with the meaning of specific gravity, the figure 2.64 indicates that the stone is two and sixty-four hundredths times as heavy as the amount of water it displaces. In other words, a cubic inch of that stone would weigh 2.64 times as much as a cubic inch of water. Hardness is determined on what we call the Mohs' scale. Let me tell you what that means."

I braced myself. I am not a scientific-minded person. What I needed most was to learn how to tell the materials by their appearances. Except for a very few people I am afraid this is true of most of us collectors. When there is really doubt about a snuff bottle substance we are content to leave it to the Gemological Institute.

"You had better look out," I said laughing. "You may find that I am like the little girl whose aunt gave her a book about penguins. Later the aunt asked her how she liked the book. 'Well, I read it,' she answered, 'but it really told me a lot more about penguins than I really wanted to know.' "

My collector friend laughed, but there was reproof, too, in his glance. "If you are going to be a serious collector of snuff bottles you have got to know some of the fundamentals about them. You understood about the specific gravity, now let me briefly explain how hardness is determined. There's a lot of difference among the stones in their resistance to abrasion, that is, in their hardness. Around 1800 a mineralogist named Mohs worked out a scale of hardness that has been in use to this very day. I've brought the scale with me. Take your bottles for testing to the Gemological Institute of America. Its main office is here in Los Angeles though there are branches in New York and other large cities. Most collectors take or send their doubtful bottles to them. But you'd better understand, however, what this Mohs scale is about. It is only a scale of ten, talc being taken as the softest and numbered one and the diamond as the hardest and numbered ten. Here's the list."

I copied it down hastily and have always kept it in my files. I confess it has considerably increased my understanding when I take bottles to be tested. At least I know something about what has to be determined about the material of a bottle.

NO. 10. CINNABAR LACQUER. In this type the Chinese surpassed the Japanese lacquerer. Named from the vermilion color in which usually found. Layer upon layer built up, then carved without possibility of correction. See page 35.

1.	talc	6.	feldspar
2.	gypsum	7.	quartz
3.	calcite	8.	topaz
4.	fluorite	9.	corundum
5.	apatite	10.	diamond

"When we say that a bottle has the hardness of 7 we mean that it won't scratch quartz, nor can it be scratched by quartz. The scale numbers indicate only the order of hardness. We mustn't suppose, for instance, that diamond (10) has twice the hardness of apatite (5), or that topaz (8) has four-fifths the hardness of diamond. As a matter of fact, the books tell us that the degree of hardness between diamond and corundum is far greater than that between corundum and talc, the softest of mineral substances. Do you see what I mean? The scale has no quantitative significance."

I thought I understood. "If our jadeite and our quartz bottles have a hardness of 7, pretty far up on that scale of ten, there isn't any danger of their breaking if we should accidentally drop them then, is there?"

My friend laughed. "You'd better not try it! You would be surprised. I once dropped one that I was testing, dropped it on a tiled bathroom floor. It smashed to smithereens. Hardness has nothing to do with brittleness, cleavability, I think they call it in the books. All stones are more or less brittle and can be fractured by a hard enough blow."

"Did you ever find snuff in one of those inside-painted bottles and try to wash it out?" I asked.

"No, I never tried that stunt. What happened?"

"Well, it had a beautifully painted landscape inside, but the snuff powder in it bothered me. It blurred the painting. After I had shaken water in it for a minute

NOS. 11–13. GLASS IMITATIONS. The Chinese were wonder workers in glass and could produce near-perfect imitations of almost any stone. Some of these are so subtle even an experienced collector is in doubt until a test is made. A scratch is usually enough to tell, as glass is softer than stone. No. 11 simulates mutton-fat jade, No. 12 green jade, and No. 13 agate. See page 36.

to wash the snuff out there was very little landscape left. I had ruined it. But why would they put snuff in those inside-painted bottles anyway? You have told me that they came late in the making of bottles, must certainly have been made for collections and not for practical use. Surely filling them with snuff spoiled them."

"I think that is a question we'll never know the answer to. But we have wandered far afield from jade. Let's go on now to the subject of quartz," continued my collector friend. "Quartz is a family name. It covers many stones, all with the same chemical formula, the same specific gravity of approximately 2.65 and a hardness of 7. So you see the quartz stones are as hard as jadeite and even harder than nephrite. Most collectors don't seem to know this. They go on the theory that if you can't scratch it with a knife it must be jade. As a matter of fact some nephrite jade can be scratched with a good piece of steel.

"Under the name of quartz there are a great variety of stones. It's a large family. There are two groups of quartz stones, however," he went on, "the transparent, like the pure crystal, and the more or less opaque ones which are the chalcedonies. They are classified as the crystalline and the cryptocrystalline, though the more common name for the cryptocrystalline, in the books on gems and stones, would appear to be chalcedony. The collector, however, is more likely to use agate as a general name.

"Among the crystalline are the rock crystal, amethyst, smoky crystal, hair crystal, and we may include the rose quartz here, too, although it almost always occurs without any crystalline external form. Among the cryptocrystalline or chalcedony, the opaque variety, we find agate, jasper, carnelian, bloodstone, sardonyx, and onyx. Of course there are others, too, but these are the ones which the Chinese seem to use for carving. It is the impurities, the foreign substance in the quartz that gives us all these different colors. There is a quartz of indefinite bluish color which seems never to have been given any specific name and goes by the general name, chalcedony."

Later this collector sent me a list which summarized much that he had told me, and added to it. I have never found a better chart for a snuff bottle collector, and I submit it here. It was for me a wonderful source of clarification and guidance.

CLASSIFICATION OF CHINESE SNUFF BOTTLES

GROUP I. *Glass*
1. Monochrome, plain or carved
2. Painted, outside or inside
3. Cameo or overlay type
4. Mottled
5. Imitations of other stones

GROUP II. *Ceramic*
1. Porcelain: monochrome
2. Porcelain: underglaze decoration
3. Porcelain: molded or carved design
4. Porcelain: overglaze decoration
5. Pottery: stoneware etc.

GROUP III. *Stone*
1. Jade: nephrite, jadeite
2. Quartz—crystalline: rock crystal, rose quartz, amethyst, smoky crystal, hair crystal
3. Quartz—cryptocrystalline or chalcedony: agate, carnelian, jasper, moss agate, sard, sardonyx, onyx
4. Semiprecious stones: aquamarine, beryl fluorite, lapis lazuli, malachite, steatite, serpentine, tourmaline, turquoise, ruby, etc.

GROUP IV. *Organic materials*
1. amber
2. coral
3. horn, rhinoceros, buffalo

4. ivory
5. jet
6. mother-of-pearl
7. tortoise shell
8. bamboo
9. wood
10. lacquer in various types

GROUP V. *Miscellaneous*

Enamel, metal, embellished, inside-painted, etc.

If you have the start of a collection and are reasonably sure of adding to it from time to time a catalogue of what you own will give you a neat and tidy feeling. Don't wait until you have so many bottles that you have forgotten what was told you by your dealer (a translation of an inscription, perhaps), or what you paid for it.

A card catalogue is best because as time goes on you will dispose of some, when you find better examples of the same type. Then, too, because tastes differ you will trade bottles with your fellow collectors. The old cards may be discarded, new ones added, and the record kept up to date. The number of my latest bottle does not mean that I have that number of bottles in my collection. It means that that many bottles have passed through my hands. I find it less confusing than to try to replace numbers.

Each collector's catalogue card will contain the information that he cares to keep. The bottle number in the left- or right-hand upper corner will correspond to the number he has written on the bottom of the bottle, or inscribed on tape and placed on the bowl of the spoon. The classification or type of bottle should be at the top and center of the card, jade, porcelain, glass, tourmaline, inside-painted, whatever classification will make it easy to find the bottle in your card catalogue. Beneath comes a description of the bottle itself, its color, height, shape, and its decoration. Describe the material of the stopper and the collar, if there is one. In the case of the inside-painted bottles which are signed, record the name of the artist. At the base of the card comes the name of the shop or person from whom you got it and the price. This last had better be in code if you don't intend to confide your extravagances to your family. Take any one or two words which contain but ten letters, no one of which is the duplicate of any other. For our example let us use the words "trade quick."

t r a d e　q u i c k
1 2 3 4 5　6 7 8 9 0

If the cost for a bottle was $27.50 your letter code would read R U. E K. As a final touch you might add an appraisal figure. This may coincide with your

1. Round bulbous bottle
2. Ovate flattened flask
3. Ovate rounded bottle
4. Elongated ovate flattened flask
5. Pebble-shaped bottle
6. Elongated ovate rounded bottle

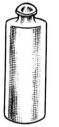

7. Cylindrical bottle with square shoulders
8. Cylindrical bottle with rounded shoulders
9. Straight-sided flattened flask
10. Melon-shaped bottle
11. "Buddha's Hand" shaped bottle
12. Pear-shaped bottle

13. Gourd-shaped bottle
14. Narrow-sided, quadrangular bottle with
    cylindrical neck
15. Flattened, spade-shaped flask
16. Pilgrim-bottle shape
17. Squat bottle of flattened spade shape

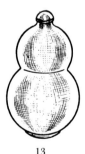

18. Baluster-shaped bottle
19. Rounded bottle bulging toward base with
    long, narrow neck
20. Animal-shaped bottle, stopper at mouth
21. Figure-shaped bottle, head for stopper
22. Twin bottles

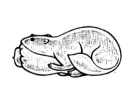

code price. Sometimes, however, you may estimate it above or below, according to your luck. At any rate, it may serve as a guide to your heirs someday if they dispose of your bottles.

No. 1	GLASS

A round bulbous bottle of brilliant raspberry red. Plain without carving. Height 2 1/2 inches. Yellow collar with fine green jade top.

Shanghai Treasures, Los Angeles TR

Appraisal $15.

My own catalogue cards have omitted the shape and height of a bottle. From this time forth I shall put them in. Identification would be easier if it were necessary, and these facts help in the visualizing of a bottle. I notice that auction catalogues usually contain them in their descriptions. The size of snuff bottles doesn't vary very much, and almost all the bottles shown here measure between 2 1/2 to 2 3/4 inches. This is why their height has not been given in the descriptions. The museums give the height of a bottle without stopper.

The shapes of bottles differ widely and take some ingenuity to describe. Borrowing from sale-catalogue terminology, let me describe a few of the more common shapes (see opposite).

In spite of a collector's scepticism in regard to reign marks on the base of snuff bottles we shall want to be able to recognize them whenever we find them. Since the use of bottles did not begin until around 1650 the first reign mark which need concern us is Shun Chih's, the first emperor of the Manchu dynasty, 1644 to 1661. We will need to be able to turn to these marks for reference from Shun Chih through the reign mark of Tao Kuang, 1821 to 1850. We might add for good measure Hsien Fêng's, 1851 to 1861, T'ung Chih's, 1862 to 1874, and Kuang Hsü's, 1875 to 1908, but we shall have little use for these late signatures except perhaps in the dating of the inside-painted bottles.

For reference I am going to include here the *nien-hao*, as they are called, both the character reign marks and also the seal marks—for these are sometimes used (see following page).

The character reign marks are usually written with six-characters and are read downwards, from right to left. The first two characters, from the right top corner down, indicate the dynasty name (the Ch'ing or Manchu dynasty). The second two, the lowest right and top left, are the important thing, the reign name. The final two characters simply denote "period made." In four-character marks

CHARACTER REIGN
MARKS

SEAL MARKS

CHARACTER REIGN
MARKS

SEAL MARKS

治年製	大清順	Chih Period Made	Great Ch'ing Shun		光年製	大清道	Kuang Period Made	Great Ch'ing Tao	
熙年製	大清康	Hsi Period Made	Great Ch'ing K'ang		豐年製	大清咸	Fêng Period Made	Great Ch'ing Hsien	
正年製	大清雍	Chêng Period Made	Great Ch'ing Yung		治年製	大清同	Chih Period Made	Great Ch'ing T'ung	
隆年製	大清乾	Lung Period Made	Great Ch'ing Ch'ien		緒年製	大清光	Hsü Period Made	Great Ch'ing Kuang	
年製	嘉慶	Period Made	Chia Ch'ing						

the only difference is the omission of the dynasty signs. The seal marks, although they appear to have no resemblance to the written marks. are in fact composed of archaic. much stylized versions of the same written characters, which, however, are more commonly arranged into three vertical columns of two characters each, as in the examples shown here. The first or right-hand column of two characters gives the dynasty name, "Great Ch'ing," the middle column consists of the two characters of the reign name, and the last or left-hand column shows "period made."

These characters are hard for a Westerner to learn and remember. I have conquered them a dozen times and forgotten them as soon as I am no longer working with them.

It is obvious, of course, that in the more commonly found character reign marks there are only two characters for us to learn out of the six. The other four are repetitions which we can ignore.

熙	大	Hsi	Great
年	清	Period	Ch'ing
製	康	Made	K'ANG

Frankly, since we are not specialists we can get along very well if we learn only the three most important of these reign marks, K'ang Hsi, Yung Chêng, and Ch'ien Lung. We can look up the others when we need them.

康	K'ang	雍	Yung	乾	Ch'ien
熙	Hsi	正	Chêng	隆	Lung

Draw these six characters every day for a while, using every mnemonic device you can think up to fix them in your mind. No matter how silly your memory tricks may be, clutch at them. For instance, at the base of the character Hsi there are four little eyes. Well, you Hsi with eyes, don't you? Let that help you. The prominent stroke in Ch'ien is ㄩ which you can easily imagine as a dog's tail. The French for dog, if you ever learned or can remember any of your French, is *chien*. When you see that tail, it's Ch'ien.

Shall I go on with my mnemonic tricks which really work? No, I'll leave you now to think up your own. They will occur to you as you copy these six characters. My sympathy is with you. They are not easy to fix. It is unkind to remind you that you'll still have the seal characters to fix in your mind. If this reduces you to desperation forget about learning them, and use this chapter as a reference.

CHAPTER FIVE

First Bottles for the Collector: The Glass

Begin with glass, if you decide to collect snuff bottles. There are good reasons for this. They are the most reasonable in price, and few of us begin by paying a hundred dollars for three inches of beauty. Such extravagance develops in us slowly.

With the prospect of acquiring the best of some fine old collection we decide to make the old car do for another year or to get along without a new suit. We are then far gone in our pursuit of snuff bottles, however. Madness such as that creeps upon us gradually. We begin by feeling that ten or fifteen dollars is quite sufficient to pay for a bottle. We are still capable of calculating comparative returns when we spend that amount in other directions. It is only later that the coin of the realm takes on an entirely different value when considered in terms of snuff bottles.

Another reason for starting with the glass bottles: we find more attractive glass bottles on the market than good ones of any other type. No matter how far you may go in your collecting, glass bottles are still to be found so lovely that you will never throw them out of your collection. If funds are limited a very enjoyable collection might be made of this type alone. Great self-restraint would have to be a quality in your make-up, however.

Glass overlay will probably be the first bottles you collect. Or they may be bottles made of the beautiful mottled glass which comes in swirls of brown and yellow and different shades of green. Then you will find amazing imitations in glass of mutton-fat jade, emerald jade, lapis lazuli, coral, agate, and many other stones.

People often give an exclamation of pleasure when I open a box holding a number of the glass-overlay or cameo-type bottles. Perhaps it is because they come in such varied combinations of color and are carved in so many different designs.

It is obvious how these bottles are made. The same technique with glass has been used in Europe as well. Sgraffito ware is similar, a kind of pottery in which

NO. 14. OVERLAY GLASS. Milk-glass bottle with an overlay. This is carved down to the basic bottle, leaving the design raised in the overlay color.

NO. 15. OVERLAY GLASS. Each flattened side overlaid with a different color, showing, respectively, the bamboo, chrysanthemum, wild orchid, and plum (shown here). See page 50.

clays of different colors are laid one upon another and the pattern produced by cutting away the outer layers. A bottle of clear milk glass, or indeed a bottle of any color whatever, is dipped in glass of another color. After this outer coat has hardened it is turned over to the carver. With his simple tools, his wheel and foot treadle, he proceeds to carve it as if it were stone. Glass is not hard. It lends itself easily to beautiful design. If a double overlay is planned the original bottle will have two layers of color applied, and the carver cuts down to the color he needs.

One of the astounding things we read in descriptions of this carving is that many a skilled craftsman works without a design. He sees it in his mind's eye as the Oriental painter must who uses his brush without possibility of correction. Occasionally we find bottles which have five or seven colors in the design. If we run our fingers over the carving we find the colors all on a level. In the double overlay bottles the second layer is always slightly higher than the first overlay. In these five- to seven-color bottles it is evident that the different colors are put on in dabs over the original bottle, all on the same level. Was the design in the carver's mind before these dabs were put on, or does he develop a design to fit them as he goes along? This we do not know.

Let me describe the overlay bottles in the box of eight before me. The picture of each bottle in color is illustrated for you. The first bottle I pick up is a milk glass with a thin overlay of black (No. 14). Bottles with this thin overlay are called seal bottles. On this type of bottle there appears almost always, along with the design, a seal mark. These milk-glass, thin-overlay bottles seem to be the only ones on which these seals appear. On the same side with the seal on this bottle the lapidary has carved the black into a flowering bush, the flower resembling a chrysanthemum. At the base of the shrub sits a little dog, with two tiny butterflies hovering over it. The outline of the bottle's base is an oval of black, and on the shoulders are carved black masks and the outline of handles in imitation of those we find on bronze vessels. On the other flattened side of the bottle (which does not appear in the picture) a fisherman under a tree on a river bank is landing a fish with his long rod. The bottle has a black collar and a green jade top.

NO. 16. OVERLAY GLASS. Startling combination of color. The overlay carved into a continuous floral design. See next page.

NO. 17. OVERLAY GLASS. The carving of the overlay down to the basic bottle done with utmost care. Sometimes, however, the carving is evident on the basic bottle. See next page.

Bottle No. 15 is also of milk glass. It is not the seal type, and the overlay is much thicker. Each of the four flattened sides has been overlaid with a different color. The four different designs, one on each panel, appear often in Chinese art and are spoken of as "the four gentlemen of China," meaning the bamboo, the chrysanthemum, the wild orchid, and the plum blossom. We meet these four in the famous old book of instruction in Chinese painting, *The Mustard Seed Garden*. I have a four panel iron-picture fire-screen, each panel of which pictures one of these themes. On this bottle the bamboo appears in an overlay of green, the chrysanthemum in orange, the wild orchid in blue, and the plum blossom in rose. The panel with the plum is the one illustrated. The bottle has no collar but a pink tourmaline top.

Bottle No. 16 is a startling combination of color, a deep-pink bottle with a yellow overlay carved in a continuous design of leaves and blossoms. It has a black collar and a green jade top.

No. 17 is a purple glass bottle with a flower design in yellow. It has a black collar and a green jade top.

No. 18 is a double overlay bottle. The bottle itself is of camphor glass, white with tiny flecks throughout which make it resemble camphor. The first overlay is of red and the second of black. In a continuous design around the bottle the lapidary has cut a relief of deer, birds, and blossoms in black, the branches and leaves in the lower layer of red. There is a black collar and a matching red glass top.

No. 19 is a brilliant blue bottle with a seal on one side. As always with the seal there is low relief carving, a thin overlay of dark red carved in a conventionalized design of "the household ornaments." There is a white collar and a top of carved ivory.

No. 20 is a milk-glass bottle with a floral design in six different colors, blue, red, green, pink, yellow, and orange. These colors must have been put on in dabs, not in different overlays, for the various colors all lie in the same plane. Once more we ask ourselves the question, did the lapidary have his design in mind when the dabs of various colors were laid on, or did he originate it to fit the colors as he found them. No collar, pale tourmaline top.

No. 21 is a camphor or snowflake-glass bottle with an overlay of brilliant red. On each side a circle of red incloses the design of trees and shrubs and some

NO. 20. OVERLAY GLASS IN SIX COLORS. The colors applied in dabs, not as consecutive overlays.

NO. 21. OVERLAY GLASS. There is carving on the overlay red, even on the rope-like encirclement of the design. Poor bottles do not have this.

NOS. 22–24. MOTTLED GLASS. The range of colors and combinations in mottled glass is endless. A group always makes a brilliant display. The gold-flecked one is particularly striking.

mythological animal. On the shoulders of the bottle is a replica in red carving of the heavy handles which appear on the bronze vessels. There is incised carving on the overlay red, even on the rope-like encirclement of the design. This places it among the best of this type of bottle, the unusual detail in the carving. There is a black collar and a green jade top. Occasionally to supply a good top the craftsman has split a mandarin bead and sunk half of it into a metal collar to form the top. You can tell from the tiny opening where a cord has passed through the bead.

Every one of these eight overlay bottles has shown a different color combination. Many others, different from those I have described and pictured, could be found in Oriental shops and in other collections.

Another favorite type among the glass bottles is the one we classify roughly as "mottled." It is as though several colors in a mixture of fluid glass were swirled around very much as the housewife stirs a mixture of chocolate into her yellow batter in making a marbled cake. Because of their startling color combinations these bottles are usually more expensive than the overlay type and we do not run across them so often.

No. 22 is mottled in flecks of purple and green. It hasn't the bold swirls of the following bottles, but it is a pleasing color combination. A black collar and a green jade top.

No. 23 is a swirl of dark brown, yellow, orange, and green. It had a yellow collar and a coral top when I first acquired it. From the way in which bottles come to us it would seem that the Oriental prefers contrasting tops for his bottles, though we can seldom be sure that the bottles have their original tops. I believe Occidentals prefer harmonizing or matching tops. At any rate I find that I have replaced the original yellow collar and coral top with a new top of harmonizing glass.

No. 24 is evenly flecked with green, gold, and black. No collar, a pink tourmaline top.

Perhaps the most interesting of all the glass bottles are those which are painted inside. But since this incredible inside-painting has been done in other materials as well, in clear crystal, in smoky crystal, in agate, and in amber bottles, I will

NOS. 25–26. MONOCHROME GLASS. We find monochrome glass in almost every color, transparent and opaque, carved and uncarved. See next page.

NO. 27. BOTTLE WITH PAINTING BETWEEN GLASS LAYERS. Although there are many inside-painted bottles, this type with the painting between two layers of glass is rare. From the collection of Arthur Loveless, Seattle. See next page.

talk about these in another chapter. Our interest is in the painting rather than the material.

There are many bottles of monochrome glass. Nos. 25 and 26 show an imperial yellow and a pink soufflé. One collection I know has a box of monochrome glass bottles each one of which is so exquisitely carved in relief that they are a delight every time I see them. Never in twenty years of search have I seen anything for sale to equal them either in color or carving. Therefore my collection contains none of them.

Twice I have come across a curious glass bottle, unusual I am sure, in which a painting is shown between two layers of glass. It has been suggested that the painting might be what we used to call as children a "transfer picture." A high-powered magnifying glass, however, reveals that it is a painting. No. 27 shows such a bottle. The covering layer of glass on this painted bottle is circular like a watch crystal.

Marcus B. Huish, in his short booklet of fifty-one pages which he calls *Chinese Snuff Bottles of Stone, Porcelain and Glass,* makes a number of comments on glass. His little book was privately printed, a single edition of 149 copies. For the first thirty-one pages he rambles on quaintly about Chinese art and philosophy in general, only in the last twenty pages settling down to the snuff bottles. Of glass he says:

"Glass was not a native invention but was brought to China as long ago as the first century of this era in the goods which enterprising travelers in the Asiatic provinces of the Roman Empire carried from Egypt and Syria to the Far East. It can well be understood that the difficulty of transport of this fragile material by land and sea rendered it of great value when it reached its destination and we cannot be surprised to find it classified with gold and precious stones. It was in the fifth century that glass was first manufactured in China and since then the art has been practiced until a perfection has been attained which not even the world-renowned Venetians have surpassed."

The Chinese do, indeed, seem to have become wonder-workers in glass. There are few of the materials of which snuff bottles are made that they have not tried to imitate in glass, including even the hornbill ivory. Of course the glassworkers have not been equally successful in imitating all types, but in some of them their imitations have been astounding.

For a long time I have had an imitation of imperial green jade that it has amused me to keep in a box with my finest jade bottles. I have enjoyed the look of astonishment that will come over a collector's face as his eye singles out that bottle. Bottles, as I have said, are just not found in imperial jade. If a collector were to be the proud owner of one of that quality he would be envied indeed. I watched the face of a man who has perhaps the finest collection in America at the present time. He looked at my bottle in amazement, then reached and took it in his hand. It was as heavy as one would expect jade to be, the glass having been weighted in some mysterious way.

"Don't look so astonished," I laughed. "I haven't anything as fine as you take that to be. It isn't jade. It's just one of the cleverest imitations in glass that I have ever seen."

CHAPTER SIX

The Quartz Bottles: A Large Family

If you make a motor trip up the West Coast, driving through Oregon you will keep noticing signs along the way that read, "Agate Shop." Many agate snuff bottles at home made me alive to these signs on such a trip, and I finally stopped at one of these shops to explore.

In the glass cases were displayed all kinds of lapidary work in agate: cuff links, rings, earrings, pendants, and many other things. I began to talk with the owner. He was a lapidary himself, but did little of the work at the present time, he said. Two or three men were kept busy at their cutting and grinding and polishing in the workshop nearby.

"Have you ever seen a Chinese snuff bottle carved out of agate?" I asked. He admitted that he had, but not for a long time. In my purse was an agate bottle I had just purchased at a favorite shop in San Francisco. It was out of its wrappings, of course, for every little while I had had to take it out and look at it. I handed it over for his inspection.

He took it to a window and looked it over carefully. He removed the stopper, and with the spoon explored the completely hollowed-out interior, hollowed out in some miraculous way even up into the shoulders. The bottle was flask like in shape, and on one of the flat surfaces, in colors differing from the bottle, there was carved in relief a spray of flowers, three varicolored blossoms and leaves, with a tiny butterfly alighting upon one of them. On the reverse side was a flowering tree, two birds in its branches and a dog lying at its base. The lapidary's face, as he turned back to me, revealed his admiration of the piece (No. 28).

"In my workshop it would take eight hours a day for more than a month to duplicate such a bottle. I now have to pay my lapidaries five dollars an hour, and everything you see in these showcases is priced according to man-hours of labor. Think how commercially impossible to attempt to make a thing like this! It would run into four figures and even then it would be just a plain bottle. My men are not artists. They could not possibly do the fine raised carving you have

here. Yet the Oriental who made this worked with a foot treadle. My men have electrically driven tools."

As he returned the bottle to me he asked, "Would you mind telling me what you had to pay for this? I've seen these before, of course. I know it was nothing compared with the amount of work spent on it."

"I paid twenty dollars for it," I laughed. "It was below average price, but even at their most expensive these are seldom more than forty or forty-five dollars —agate bottles, I mean."

"Yes, because the material is so common. We read in the books that quartz, including agate, is the most common substance on the earth's surface."

"Yes, I've just been reading that quartz makes up twelve percent of the earth's outer shell, about one-eighth of the total substance of it."

"True enough," he answered, "and that isn't guesswork either. It's the result of careful analysis by scientists, made after an extensive and painstaking sampling of all the material of the rock earth."

NO. 29. ROCK CRYSTAL. This is so pure a crystal it might easily be mistaken for glass. But, unless handled, it is cooler than glass, shows no bubbles, and will not scratch. See page 61.

NO. 30. CARVED AMETHYST. A crystalline variety of quartz to which manganese oxide gives it its color. The value of an amethyst bottle depends on its depth of color and unflawed material. See page 62.

NO. 28 a, b. CARVED AGATE. Two sides of bottle shown the owner of an Oregon agate shop who estimated the prohibitive number of hours it would take his lapidaries to produce it—without decorative carving. See previous page.

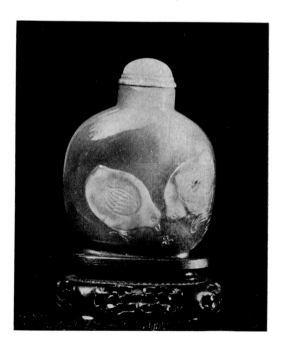

NOS. 31–35. CARVED AGATES. All specimens of carving on the cryptocrystalline or opaque form of quartz, properly called chalcedony. The ingenuity of the lapidary in using the various intrusive materials of the original stone to create the design for the bottle is truly amazing. See page 64.

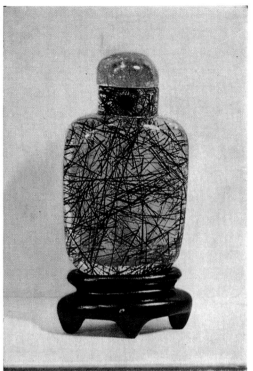

NOS. 36–38. HAIR CRYSTALS. Specimens of crystal bottles with inclusions of "needles" of rutile, which look like hairs. In No. 38 they give the appearance of seaweed at the bottom of the ocean.

I had been delving deeply into books for information on my quartz bottles and now—though I do hope it isn't telling you "more about penguins than you really want to know"—I'd like to share some of the things that I have felt were the most interesting facts about them.

Quartz is the family name for a great variety of minerals, agate included, and there seems to be an explanation for the family's forming so large a part of the earth's surface. Molten quartz has a density of 2.2 as compared with 2.65 in its solid state. This lighter density may have had a tendency to segregate the quartz toward the top of the earth's molten mass and may account for the exceeding abundance of it in the upper or outermost layers of the earth's crust.

We learn very shortly after we begin to collect quartz bottles that they fall into two categories, the crystalline and the cryptocrystalline (or chalcedony).

Among the crystalline which we find carved into bottles are the rock crystal, hair crystal, smoky crystal, and the amethyst. These are the kinds of quartz which form in definite crystals of six-sided prismatic shape. They are more or less transparent.

The other type, the cryptocrystalline, or chalcedony, is more or less opaque and includes agate, jasper, carnelian, sard, onyx, sardonyx, and many others. In this type the individual crystals are so minute that their presence can be proved only under the polarizing microscope.

Not all the chalcedony type are found in snuff bottles. I have named only those that I have seen. Considering, however, that the quartz family appears in two hundred or more forms it is understandable that quartz bottles, new in appearance, may always be turning up.

Among the coarsely crystalline bottles the rock crystal is pure silicon dioxide, free of all coloring matter. I remember well my first rock-crystal bottle (No. 29). It was so pure a crystal that it might easily have been mistaken for glass. In fact it was so mistaken by a dealer in Oriental art who sat beside me at an auction on the day that I had acquired it. I had a habit, in those days of first enthusiasm, of carrying my latest treasure around with me in my purse. I pulled it out and showed it to him.

"Surely you don't think that is crystal, do you? It's glass. Crystal is cool to the touch. This has no coolness."

Doubts immediately beset me. Certainly the bottle had no coolness. I was not aware then as I am now that a coolness beyond that of glass almost at once leaves a crystal bottle when it has been held in warm hands. This dealer should have known, too, that I need not have taken it to the Gemological Institute for testing, as I immediately did. We could have settled the matter on the spot as to whether it were glass or crystal by attempting to scratch the bottom of it with the point of a steel knife. The bottle could not be scratched. It was pure rock crystal.

Smoky quartz bottles exist in all gradations from the merest tinge of color to some so dense as to be practically black and opaque. This would depend on the amount of carbonaceous and organic matter in its substance. The transparent bottles of medium smokiness are the most beautiful and almost all collections have them.

The hair-crystal bottles are pure rock crystal with the inclusion of "needles" of rutile, slender crystals which look like hairs. The distribution of these hairs differs so greatly that few of us are satisfied with one example. The range is wide, from delicate to bold criss-crossing of rutile. (Nos. 36 and 37) The favorite among my own is a pebble-shaped crystal bottle with a chance arrangement of the hairs that resembles some formation in nature, seaweed at the bottom of the ocean perhaps (No. 38). Sometimes the hairs are of tourmaline and we get a red hair crystal.

We find the rose-quartz bottles varying from pale pink to deep rose. The inclusion which gives the color is said to be a small amount of the salts of titanium. These bottles are often flawed by milky whiteness, such defects bringing out the lapidary's ingenuity, as he seeks to conceal them by carving. I have yet to find

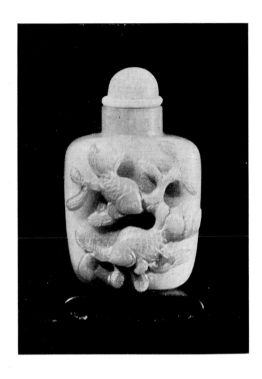

NOS. 39–40. CARVED AGATES. Two examples. In the first a thick layer of carnelian against a light brown base has resulted in a high relief carving of goldfish and seaweed. In No. 40 the base is dark green, with the design in brown. See page 65.

my ideal rose-quartz bottle, of fine even color, unflawed, standing on its own merits as a perfect stone, without benefit of any carving whatever.

Collectors who keep their bottles in cabinets instead of in boxes are warned that the color in rose quartz seems fugitive, and long exposure to sunlight will greatly fade it. I have heard, however, that if placed in a dark, humid place for some time the depth of color returns. Why this is so poses an interesting question for some mineralogist to solve.

The value of an amethyst bottle, too, depends on unflawed material and depth of color. The inclusion here which gives the amethyst color is manganese oxide. My own example, though finely carved throughout its surface, seems not to have been so treated to conceal flaws. I have had it for a long time and felt no temptation to replace it (No. 30).

As rock crystal seems to make a good starting point in enumerating varieties of crystalline bottles, so chalcedony gives a point of departure in the discussion of the cryptocrystalline. In fact it gives its name to all this minutely crystalline group, which includes agate, jasper, carnelian, sard, onyx, sardonyx, and many others.

At this point I want to point out again that gemologists consistently refer to this opaque type of quartz, the cryptocrystalline, as chalcedony, not as agate. On the other hand, the layman, in fact all the collectors I know, use the term agate to describe the various types of opaque quartz. Our boxes of "agate" bottles will include every type of chalcedony. The shops along the highways of Oregon, which I have already mentioned, are always called "agate" shops, although the carved and polished stones they handle will include every type of chalcedony, of which, strictly speaking, agate is only one. In fact, the scientific definition of agate would limit it to a banded chalcedony in which the bands of different colors are curved.

Shall we collectors obstinately continue our incorrect nomenclature or align ourselves with the scientists and refer to our many types of opaque quartz bottles as chalcedony? I myself feel inclined to fall in line with the scientists, but I am sure I shall be bringing upon myself the burden of a sort of crusade if I should persist on this point. The first collector with whom I use the term chalcedony will be sure that I am using the term to refer to the light bluish grey bottles for which the scientists use the term in its specialized sense. All this is confusing, and perhaps the gemologists on their part should reform a bit and refrain from using chalcedony both in a general and in a specialized sense.

If we snuff bottle collectors are confused by this double use of the term it is

NOS. 41–42. CARVED AGATES. The intrusive material in chalcedony appears in contrasting colors, offering a challenge to the carver in his creation of a design.

NO. 43. ONYX. When we get a deep black background with a white layer superimposed and carved in cameo fashion we call it onyx. White against carnelian or sard is called sardonyx. See page 65.

comforting to know that the gemologists themselves are aware of this confusion. One mineralogist declares that the terms agate and chalcedony are often used loosely and interchangeably and that "where to cease calling chalcedony agate and vice versa is a matter of debate and personal opinion." Dana, the famous mineralogist, refers to agate as "a variegated chalcedony," which implies that some pattern or markings must be present. Certainly, among the stones commonly called agate we find a great diversity of color, mixtures, and shades, the most common being red, brown, yellow, green, blue, grey, and black.

Let me describe five agates in my collection of a kind I especially like. On the body of the bottles inclusions of different colors have been utilized to carve in relief whatever has been suggested by the contrasting material.

On the first (No. 31) is a dappled deer poised on a rock. On No. 32 is a bird on a bush with a butterfly almost in reach of his bill. On No. 33 is a cat and two butterflies. No. 34 has an eagle in lighter material carved against a darker background. On a rich, reddish bottle (No. 35) inclusions of decided yellow have been carved into two chickens. There is a marvel of imagination and ingenuity in the use of intrusive material. The included contrasting substance is not removed. It offers challenge and is utilized.

Besides these inclusions where design can be made in low or in no relief, there

NOS. 44–45. PUDDING STONE. A conglomerate jasper cemented into a compact mass by chalcedony or some other quartz material is called pudding stone by collectors. No two are ever alike. See page 67.

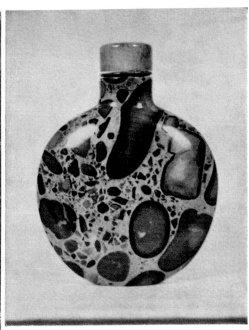

NO. 46. MOSS AGATE. Named after the moss- or fern-like inclusions found usually in rather colorless chalcedony. They are the result of iron and other impurities.

NO. 47. "MACARONI" AGATE. Streamers of milky quartz enclosed in chalcedony, the macaroni-like circular openings at the ends suggesting the name to collectors. See next page.

NO. 48. PUDDING STONE. Another example showing the range in forms and colors found in these stones. See page 67.

are often layers of contrasting color of such depth that, like the glass-overlay bottles, the designs in cameo fashion can be carved in high relief. No. 39 shows a light-brown bottle with an overlay of carnelian on which have been carved two fish in motion amid seaweed. High relief of brown against a dark green gives us the deep carving of a monkey, tree, ram, and bird of No. 40. Of this kind, too, designs are endless.

When we get a deep black background on which a white layer is superimposed and carved in cameo fashion we call them onyx bottles. On the black bottle shown (No. 43) the carved overlay is slightly more grey than white. These are striking bottles on account of the sharply contrasting colors. Where a white layer is contrasted with a background of carnelian or sard the combination is called sard-onyx.

No. 46 shows a moss agate. These moss agates are pleasing. They take their name from the moss-, fern-, or tree-like inclusions found usually in rather color-

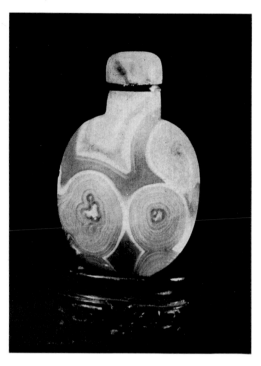

NO. 49. BANDED OR "FORTIFICATION" AGATE. The banded lines may be roughly parallel or deposited in an angular manner suggesting an aerial view of old fortifications.

NO. 50. QUARTZ. A startling specimen with a design of concentric rings suggesting petrified wood or some fossil-like formation.

less chalcedony. These inclusions of red, green, or brown are due to iron or some other substance present as an impurity.

There are bottles hollowed paper-thin of a mixture of colors which resemble tortoise shell. One such bottle in my collection discloses a tragedy. The poor lapidary, after weeks of slow work with his disk and abrasives, had continued his paring down of material a moment too long. His tool broke through the transparency of the bottle! What tragedy after all those weeks of labor! Just another of life's little ironies that that ruined piece of craftsmanship is now a collector's prized bottle. The lapidary had plugged the break-through with a bit of silver.

Carnelian bottles are often mixed with other chalcedony colors. The red carnelian color is due to small amounts of impurities in the form of oxides of iron hematite. My own carnelian is an uncarved bottle of pure, brilliant, even color.

No doubt bloodstone bottles exist, translucent dark-green plasma containing spots of bright blood jasper. The green color is probably due to chlorite, possibly ferrous iron salts, the red to hematite. One of my bottles reverses the colors, the basic color is red, the spots green.

There are bottles the collectors call "macaroni" agate (No. 47). Against a chalcedony background are streamers of milky quartz the endings of which appear with circular openings like macaroni. Milky quartz itself is said to be due to no coloring matter, but to millions of fluid inclusions. Though I have found nothing described or named as "macaroni" quartz in any of the books, most collectors have this type of bottle, however.

Pudding-stone bottles are a dramatic type. This is a conglomerate jasper cemented into a compact mass by chalcedony or some other quartz mineral. In some of the bottles it appears like pebbles caught in a matrix. No two are ever alike. Nos. 44, 45, and 48 are pudding-stone bottles.

Large collections in which a collector has tried to get every type usually contain a banded or "fortification" agate, as it is called. The lines of banding, of different shades, may be roughly parallel (No. 49), or deposited in an angular manner as though to represent an aerial view of old fortifications.

No. 50 shows a startling bottle of light-brown background on which are scattered ovals with white outline within which are innumerable concentric rings. These ovals resemble pictures of petrified wood or fossil formation. As yet I have no name for this, though one instinctively knows that the bottle is some form of quartz. In fact, though quartz appears in so many forms it seems one of the easiest of minerals for the experienced collector to identify. Any mineral which possesses a glassy to waxy lustre, which has average gravity when sufficiently hollowed out, and which will scratch glass easily but cannot be scratched in turn, is most likely to be quartz. It has a cool feeling not possessed by glass, but loses this quickly by handling. I have described the commonest, but by no means all, of the quartz bottles.

CHAPTER SEVEN

Porcelain Bottles: A Lifetime Study

Knowledge of Chinese porcelain requires a unique experience. One may delve into all the literature ever written on this subject, yet one must have the opportunity to view, handle, and discuss the actual products of this great handicraft with some knowledgeable person. Otherwise, no authoritative judgment will be possible.

In addition to this, it is the individual who has dabbled a bit in the making of ceramics himself who most surely develops that sixth sense necessary for genuine knowledge of Chinese porcelain. He must have actually worked with the "bones" (the quarried rock), the "body" (the kneaded clay), and the "skin" (the marvellously manipulated enamels). There are not many in this country who can qualify.

I approach this chapter with reluctance, certainly with humility. I should need another lifetime in which to know porcelains. Yet great numbers of our snuff bottles are made of this ware. Some writers believe that they were the first containers used for snuff, a carry-over from the previously made perfume bottles and miniature vases. Certainly the porcelain bottles exist in great variety. Among them we find the painted, enameled, overglazed and underglazed, carved, molded, incised, reticulated, and among many monochrome glazes there are crackles, soufflés, flambés, blanc de chines, mirror blacks, clair de lunes, and peach blooms. Even with this long list there may have been omissions.

Perhaps the history of Chinese porcelain in its most flourishing period, the Manchu dynasty, might be told in these miniatures, the snuff bottles, if we could ever get them together. It is the period, at least, which coincides with the time when snuff bottle production was at its height. If we were to add the miniature vases, the cosmetic and medicine jars of earlier periods, which were later converted into snuff bottles, we might considerably extend the scope.

Those who have been collectors for years will recognize by name all the bottles on the long list which has been given. But to know for a certainty in whose reign they were made, to date them, in fact, is quite another matter. We are warned that the reign marks mean nothing. When the Chinese copied an early and fine piece of porcelain they copied the mark as well. That is well understood. They may be copying some of the earliest porcelain snuff bottles today for all we know. And since at the present time the "bamboo curtain" prevents any enterprising collector from going into China with the determination to find out, we are not likely to date them with any assurance. The making of fine porcelain is probably as little a lost art in China as the making of the wonderful old lacquer is in Japan. But both saw their development in a leisured day in which time did not count. Today it has become commercially inexpedient to produce them.

In spending thirty or forty dollars for an interesting porcelain bottle—unless we are in close touch (as is unlikely) with the few qualified experts on porcelain in this country—we collectors have but two things to guide us: to use all our native and acquired artistic sense to assure us that the piece has intrinsic beauty and to be able to rely somewhat upon the dealers from whom we purchase. I qualify this last because I do not believe that many Oriental dealers really know their porcelains. There are too many other things in their business which they have to know. But let's be sure of their sincerity and of their greater opportunity than ours to make contact with those who know.

The purchase, for any large sum, of a porcelain bottle is the most precarious in our range of buying. The hours and hours of labor that have gone into the making and carving of the quartz and semiprecious-stone bottles are self-evident. With improving living conditions and the rising cost of labor throughout the world such workmanship will soon be prohibitive in cost. We need hardly fear to gamble on the current price of a stone bottle. So, too, with the *laque burgauté*, high priced though they are. They speak eloquently for the artistry, craftsmanship, and infinite patience which went into their production. We may feel the same if we count up the costs in the making of a fine embellished piece, the carving of the original jade bottle, the skill that has gone into the manipulation of the semiprecious stones in the forming of human figures and other elements in its design. Take, also, the very best of the bottles carved of wood. They equal the finest of the Japanese *netsuke*. In these, and in many other types, we know we are getting full value.

Now hold in your hand a monochrome porcelain. If you have ever followed the work of the modern ceramic makers in America does not the doubt sting your mind that they could reproduce this piece? How much more easily it could be reproduced in the country in which it originated. Since these porcelains bring good prices in America why should Orientals not have continued to reproduce them? And if reproducible at all, why not in quantity?

Of late years I have grown more cautious in my purchases of porcelain bottles than of any other type. I cannot give that necessary "part of a lifetime" to acquiring knowledge. I confess, however, that occasionally my scepticism weakens. Not before a monochrome, pleasing as it often is. With long enough training in the ceramist's art and with enough patience conceivably I might make one of them myself. Nor does it weaken before a porcelain decorated with formalized or geometric design. That, also, does not exceed a good copyist's skill. Before a porcelain, however, on which a miniature landscape has been painted in the tradition of great Chinese painting, before such a piece humbly I admit that fine porcelain bottles may yet be found. Intrinsically the value is there, and I care not whether it was made yesterday (which I doubt) or in the time of Ch'ien Lung as it is claimed.

If Mr. Hitt had lived to write his second book on snuff bottles it would have had much greater value for us than his first. After my visit to him at Bremerton there was considerable correspondence between us about the bottles. He was feeling his way, but he was a good researcher. In one letter he writes, "This year I have enrolled for a University of Washington course in Oriental Ceramic Art under Dr. Sherman Lee. The two-hour class will be held at the Seattle Art Museum, with all its treasures at our disposal for study. Dr. Lee calls it, 'The Aesthetics and Identification of Oriental Ceramics,' but he will give us all the technical end of how they were made. Professor Bonifas, who teaches all the ceramic classes at University of Washington will be one of us. I expect to get a lot out of this." I haven't a doubt that he did. I was envious as he described their sessions.

Later he sent me carbons of some of his correspondence with Mr. Henry Muell of Detroit, a snuff bottle collector, working in ceramics, and actually trying to reproduce Chinese snuff bottles. It is evident from the letters and from the outfit which Mr. Muell sent to him that Mr. Hitt was making some attempt with ceramics himself. He was fitting himself with all the qualifications I have mentioned for knowing porcelains. He had read widely on his subject, his university course at the museum was giving him the viewing and handling of porcelains under knowledgeable direction, he was even meeting that deeper requirement of coming to grips with the problem of its production at first hand. Had he lived we would have had a wonderful chapter on porcelain snuff bottles, one that I cannot write for you.

One letter to Mr. Muell contains considerable material that he might have given us in his second book. In such researches we build upon the knowledge which has been gleaned for us by others, and I can do nothing better than to give you his long letter in full.

He quotes at length from the description of porcelain making, written in 1712, by Père d'Entrecolles, the Jesuit missionary. He adds the account written in

1743 by T'ang Ying, the celebrated director of the imperial porcelain factory at Ching Tê Chên. "This covers," he says "all the first-hand information we have of Chinese porcelain modeling. Accounts in various other books all apparently spring from these two sources."

What follows in the letter is his own personal reconstruction of the information as applied to snuff bottles. It is a valuable letter and tells us much about the making of the bottles.

Bremerton, Washington, July 21, 1949

My dear Mr. Muell,—

Thank you for your good letter, and the promise that when you get your home-cooked bottles out of storage you will let me have some examples. I would certainly like to talk glazes with you, but it is too big a subject to get into a letter. I would like much to learn how you mold your bottles. In order to clarify my own ideas on how the Chinese probably mold snuff bottles, and draw out comments from you and others, I will now break into a bit of a thesis:

The only first-hand accounts of how they do it are in the pertinent part of a letter from the Jesuit missionary, Père d'Entrecolles. After describing the mixture he writes, 'From such elements are produced many beautiful works of porcelain, some fashioned upon the wheel, others made by molds, and finished afterward with the polishing knife.

'The plain, round pieces are all fashioned on the wheel. A cup, when it comes off the wheel, is very imperfectly shaped. The foot is only a piece of clay of the diameter that it is intended to have ultimately, and it is not excavated with the knife until all other operations are finished. The cup, as it comes from the wheel, is first handed to a second workman who is seated beneath. It is passed by him to a third who presses it on a mold and gives it shape; this mold is fixed upon a sort of wheel. A fourth workman polishes the cup with a knife, especially around the rims, and makes it thin enough to be transparent. Each time he scrapes it, it must be moistened carefully or it will break. It is surprising to see the rapidity with which the vases pass through so many hands, and I am told that a vase that has been fired has gone through the hands of seventy workmen.

'Large objects of porcelain are made in two pieces; one half is lifted upon the wheel by three or four men, who support it on each side while it is being shaped; the other half is fitted upon the first when it is sufficiently dried, and it is cemented to it with a porcelain earth mixed with water (that is, a slip) which serves as mortar or glue. When quite dry the place of juncture is pared with a knife, inside and outside, so that, after glazing, there remains no inequality of surface. Handles, ears and similar adjuncts are attached by means of slip in the same way. This refers principally to the porcelain which is made in molds, or by handwork, such as fluted pieces, or those of bizarre shape, such as animals, grotesques, idols, the busts ordered by Europeans, and such like. These objects, when molded, are made in three or four pieces, which are fitted together, and finished afterward with instruments adapted for excavating, polishing, and working the various details that have escaped the mold. As for flowers and ornaments which are not in relief, but, as it were, in intaglio, these are impressed on the porcelain with seals and molds. Reliefs, ready prepared, are also put on porcelain in the same way almost as gold lace is attached to a coat.

'I have lately investigated the subject of these molds. When the mold of the piece of porcelain to be made is at hand, and it is such as cannot be shaped upon the wheel by the potter, they press upon the mold some yellow clay, specially prepared for molding. The clay is impressed in this way, the mold being composed of several pieces of pretty large size, which are left to harden when they have been properly impressed. When they are used they are put near the fire for some time, and then filled with porcelain earth to the thickness the piece is to have, and this is pressed into every part with the hands. The mold is held to the fire for a moment, to detach the "squeeze" from the mold. The different pieces which have been separately molded in this way are joined together afterward with a slip. I have seen animals of massive proportions fabricated by these means. After the mass has been left to harden it is worked into the desired form, and finished with the chisel. Finally, each of the parts worked separately is adjusted. When the object has been finished off with great care the glaze is put on, and it is then fired.'

This ends the molding description.

We also have the descriptions written in 1743 by T'ang Ying, the celebrated director of the imperial porcelain manufactory at Ching Tê Chên, of twenty paintings of porcelain manufacture that had been made at some earlier date. They are published by Bushell in *Oriental Ceramic Art*.

Illustration number 5 shows the preparation of the molds. No. 6 shows the fashioning of round ware on the wheel, and T'ang Ying describes it: 'There are several different processes of work in the manufacture of this round ware. The square, polygonal, and ribbed pieces, and those with projecting corners, have to be carved and finished with the polishing knife, all of which are different branches of work.

'The plain round pieces are turned on the wheel, being distributed according to their size between two classes of workmen. The first takes the large pieces— the second, takes on the wheel the same kind of pieces which measure less than a foot across. The wheel consists of a disk of wood, mounted below upon a perpendicular axle, so as to revolve continuously for a long time, during which the piece must be properly turned without becoming too thick, too thin, flattened or otherwise misshapen. There is a carpenter at hand to repair it when necessary.

'Beside the wheel is an attendant workman who kneads the paste to a proper consistency and puts it on the table. The potter sits upon the border of the framework and turns the wheel with a bamboo staff. While the wheel is spinning round he works the paste with both hands. It follows the hands, lengthening or shortening, contracting or widening, in a succession of shapes. It is in this way the round ware is fashioned so that it varies not a hair's breadth in size.

'Illustration number 7 describes the manufacture of vases: The plain round vases are fashioned upon the potter's wheel in the same manner as the ordinary ware. They are then dried in the open air and turned on the polishing wheel to be finished with the knife. In making the carved, polygonal, ribbed, and fluted vases the paste, wrapped in cotton cloth, is pressed with flat boards into thin slabs which are cut with knives into sections. The pieces are joined together with a slip cement made of some of the original paste with water. There is another kind of vase which is made with the process of molding, and which is finished after it is taken from the mold in the same way. The carved polygonal vases and the carved molded vases have to be filled and washed clean with the brush in the same way as the round vases turned upon the wheel.

'All the varied forms of vases may be engraved with the style, or embossed in relief, or carved in open-work designs, for which purposes, when sufficiently dried, they are given to artificers specially devoted to these several branches of work.

'After the large and small pieces have been shaped on the wheel, and have been sufficiently dried in the air, they are put into the molds which have been previously prepared and are pressed gently with the hands until the paste becomes of regular form and uniform thickness. The piece is then taken out and dried in a shady place till it is ready to be shaped with the polishing knives.

'Illustration number 14 shows turning the unbaked ware and scooping out the foot. The size of the round piece has been fixed in the mold, but the smooth polish of the surface depends upon the polisher, whose province is another branch of work, that of "turning." He uses in his work the polishing wheel which in form is like the ordinary potter's wheel, only it has projecting upward in the middle a wooden mandrel, the size of which varies, being proportioned to that of the porcelain which is about to be turned. The top of this mandrel which is rounded is wrapped in raw silk to protect the interior of the piece from injury. The piece about to be turned is put upon the mandrel, the wheel is spun around and it is pared with the knife until both the inside and the outside are given the same perfectly smooth finish. . . . With regard to the next process, that of scooping out the foot, it is necessary because each piece when first fashioned upon the potter's wheel, has a paste handle left under the foot two or three inches long, by which it is held while it is being painted and the glaze blown on. It is only after the glazing and the painting of the decoration are finished that this handle is removed by the polisher, who at the same time scoops out the foot, after which the mark is written underneath.'

.That about covers all the first-hand information we have of Chinese porcelain modeling. Accounts in various other books are taken from these two sources. And more is hardly needed. We have an excellent picture, except that much of it does not apply to our small snuff bottles. But we find that this gives us many clues to how they are formed and put together from different molded pieces, as we have seen is frequently done with larger pieces.

What follows is my own personal reconstruction, and I cordially invite discussion of it.

First I will divide all our snuff bottles into round bottles and those which are not round. By round, I mean, of course, round in plan, whether cylindrical, globose, or vase shaped, shapes that could be formed on a potter's wheel. Not round will include all the flattened flask-shaped bottles, square bottles and all odd shapes.

I believe that practically all our snuff bottles of ceramics are shaped in external molds, either the whole bottle or parts of it. This applies to both round and not-round types. And we have seen that nearly all Chinese porcelain is rough thrown on the potter's wheel, shaped in a revolving mold, dried, and then finished with a polishing knife.

Let us first consider the cylindrical bottles, usually dated as K'ang Hsi, and similar shapes. These are, I am sure, molded with the base open. They often show a spiral inside where the rough bottle off the potter's wheel has been forced out against an external mold. In the case of the cylindrical mold it would be loose after the clay had dried a bit. Molds for other shapes would be in halves. The base, separately turned would finally be added. The stopper end may have been molded with the exterior, or was a separate piece. While the joint at the bottom is often indicated by a swelling or irregularity I have been unable to detect a joint at the top. In any case, the exterior would all be finished finally with the potter's knife, with especial attention to the top flange and opening before firing.

Many of the miniature vases of the seventeenth century and earlier that have been converted into snuff bottles were probably made in one piece, following the routine our two authorities have described. They had an opening large enough to allow the use of molding tools on both the potter's wheel and the polishing wheel, and revolving external molds. Their foot was probably cut off as described by T'ang Ying, though I doubt if any regular small-mouthed bottles, snuff bottles, had this operation performed. One of my finest bottles, a blue underglaze, is wide-mouthed and shows a near spiral inside, starting in the middle of the bottom and twisting up the sides evidently made with a blunt tool crowding the clay out against the external mold. I have a curious little bottle entirely unfired and finished with drawings under a wax coating where the base came off and showed the potter's finger marks all over the interior of the bottle, pressing it out into a mold before the base was stuck on.

Another method of forming round bottles was to split them longitudinally half-way up. The bottom section and the upper section were separately formed as just described for miniature vases, and these are joined to make the bottle. Probably the gourd-shaped bottles were made this way. In some cases the joint was left to plainly show on the outside, but usually it was entirely polished off.

That covers my surmise as how round bottles were formed, and brings us to the not-rounds that include most of our ceramic snuff bottles. A great many of these show clearly how they were made, showing an evident joining all the way up the thin sides. On others there is no sign of this joint, but I believe they were all so made. Two halves were made in open molds simply by pressing the clay in and letting it dry. The joint was then ground smooth and they were cemented together with slip and further sealed by the glaze later. In some cases tops and bottoms were separately molded pieces, sometimes not, the seam showing across the bottom.

This procedure, of course, allowed for any desired exterior shape including many of the carved designs, by simply having the molds the right shape (any undercutting of the design would be done as the bottle was smoothed up with a potter's knife). If the two sides of a bottle are the same they will usually be found identical in every little detail. Both sides were molded from the same mold.

Square and flat panel bottles were probably made as just described. The reticulated ones present some interesting puzzles. They are evidently built up through several operations of which carving is not one. The inner bottle was probably made in two halves as usual. Then this was covered with some sand mixture or silk fibre that would disintegrate in light firing later. Over this the reticulated layer of clay, formed in a mold, was placed. Then on top of this the various little designs, all molded as is evidenced by their being identical in every detail, were stuck on. After thorough drying the various glazes were put on and the whole was fired. Clay suitable for this molding and sticking on is evidently fragile, for these bottles do not wear well. Many come to us with expert repairs.

Some of our loveliest bottles are very delicately and wonderfully carved on clay added to the outside of regularly formed bottles. These often show the joining seams on the sides with the beautifully carved design on added clay running right across it. It is puzzling why, for such wonderful bottles, they let the joining patch show. Some Chinese quirk. The carving on these bottles is often masterful

NOS. 51–53. I-HSING POTTERY. These bottles take their name from the province where they were made. We find them painted (No. 51), carved in relief (No. 52), and enameled (No. 53). The last is from the Seattle Art Museum. See page 79.

and original. They are not molded, though some dragon designs are standard. They are often blanc de chine. The finest of them show a very interesting signature on the base, sharply standing up in relief. Evidently these bases were molded separately, and these fine bottles do not show the side seams as do some others.

That is the story of molding Chinese snuff bottles as I see it at the present writing. I am interested in any and all comments on the above. You have actually been making bottles, whereas I am all surmise and reading. Please sail into me with both feet wherever you think I am wrong. I shall like it.

Yours truly,

Henry Hitt

Some snuff bottle collectors may feel that in this quoted letter there is "a great deal more about penguins than we really want to know." Inexperienced in ceramics as I am, I felt that way myself the first time I read it. Yet, in writing this book, I decided that this condensed description of the processes of porcelain making should be made available to those who *did* want to know. My experience has been that, having read the letter when first received, with little visualization of what Mr. Hitt quotes and describes, having read it again with the feeling that it ought to be incorporated here, having copied it into my manuscript, and read it again to compare it with the original, at long last I began to understand what it was all about. I find I cannot look at my boxes of porcelain bottles now without the added appreciation of perceiving how they were made. It is an added dimension of enjoyment. I can only recommend that you study the letter.

The very name "china" gives credit to the fact that the ware originated in that country. The West has never laid claim to it. The period during which there was greatest activity in the making of snuff bottles coincides with the great revival in porcelain manufacture which began after the establishment of the Manchu dynasty and the rebuilding of Ching Tê Chên. This famous porcelain center had been destroyed in the rebellions which marked the change of dynasties.

Ching Tê Chên and its neighborhood had long been noted for its excellent ceramic wares. All that the industry required in the way of material was lavishly supplied by the neighboring hills, *kaolin* (china clay for the body of the porcelain) and *petuntse* (china stone) to mix with it and to form the glaze, wood ashes to soften the glaze, and cobaltiferous ore of manganese to make the blue for the underglaze painting and the blue glazes. When, in his desire to encourage every field of the arts K'ang Hsi established twenty-seven imperial workshops in his capital, the manufacture of porcelain alone was given up and returned to its old center. The difficulty of transportation of materials had proved to be too great.

Père d'Entrecolles, who lived at Ching Tê Chên for a number of years in the early part of the eighteenth century, has given us a vivid description of the town as it was in its most flourishing state. Its population was estimated at a million, all—even the blind and crippled—engaged in some capacity connected with the porcelain industry. Its three thousand kilns blazed at night with the semblance of a town on fire. Division of labor prevailed to an extent scarcely outdone by the most modern industrial organization. Throwing, molding, assembling of parts, the painting of the various subjects, each was the concern of a separate workman. One piece, he tells us, as Mr. Hitt quotes in his letter, would sometimes pass through the hands of seventy workmen.

True porcelain is distinguished from earthenware by certain qualities. It should be so hard that steel will not scratch it, should be free from any porous quality, and when chipped should show that it is brilliantly white throughout its substance. It should be resonant, vitrified so as to give a musical note when struck. The qualities of whiteness and translucency are included as characteristic.

We find snuff bottles made of pottery in which these porcelain qualities are absent. They are usually called I-hsing bottles, taking their name from the prov-

NOS. 54–56. UNDERGLAZE BLUE-AND-WHITE PORCELAIN. The design was painted on before the glaze was applied. Confident dating of these bottles is almost impossible. No. 54 is from the collection of Russell Mullin, Beverly Hills. See pages 82–83.

NO. 57 (below). UNDERGLAZE BLUE-AND-WHITE PORCELAIN. A superb bottle, possibly made in the K'ang Hsi period, when the best porcelain was produced. From the collection of Arthur Loveless, Seattle. See page 82.

NO. 58. UNDERGLAZE RUST PORCELAIN. Found less often than the blues, it is considered among collectors to have been difficult to fire successfully. See page 83.

ince in which they are made. We find them painted like No. 51, carved in relief like No. 52, and enameled like No. 53, and they are often attractive bottles. There is nothing about them, however, that indicates that they might not have been made yesterday. That fact, fortunately, is usually reflected in the price we are asked to pay for them.

The making of I-hsing pottery dates back to an earlier period than the Manchu dynasty, probably the second half of the Ming. It developed because of a fine deposit of clay nearby and was used for utility purposes rather than for art objects. Its teapots were famous. Snuff bottles may have been made for use early in the days of snuff taking, and their production may have continued till the present day as other pottery objects have been. Once in a while an I-hsing bottle

NOS. 59–60. CARVED AND MOLDED POR-CELAIN. No. 59 has the frequently used "hundred antiques" design, with an incised background called "graviata." The design of a dragon appears on the reverse of No. 60. See page 83.

looks old. It may only have been much-used. I doubt anyone's ability to date them.

Near the start of my chapter I gave a long list of the many types of porcelain bottles. Among the illustrations you will find an example of almost every one of these. Where there have been omissions it is because, as in the case of incised bottles, photography has failed to do the bottle justice.

Nos. 54, 55, and 56 show three bottles of underglazed blue. The blue design has been painted before the glaze has been applied. This type of work had been done in much earlier times than the snuff bottle era, but a different blue had been used and a different technique in design. In the archaizing of art objects that seems to have taken place in all periods, bottles in Ming design and color were probably made, but we know the bottles were not made or used in the Ming period.

W. B. Honey, in his *Guide to the Later Porcelain* has this to say: "By the time of K'ang Hsi the Chinese had learned to refine the local mineral (which produced the blue) and on most of the porcelain of his reign it appears as a blue of remarkable depth and purity, applied in graded washes over slight outlines, remarkably different from the single tone color and bold outlines of the commoner Ming styles. Whilst the mark of K'ang Hsi is not at all common on wares dating from his reign, those of Ch'eng Hua, Hsuan Te and Chia Ching (of the earlier dynasty) are frequently found, though we know they could not have been produced at that time. The color naturally varied to some extent but even export wares of the least pretentious kind rarely show K'ang Hsi blue of poor quality. It is to the color that the critic, Chinese or Western, will first of all turn when appraising a piece of blue and white porcelain.

"The first twenty years of the 18th century may be regarded as the culminating period in the technical development of the blue and white porcelain. In the second decade of the century its place began to be taken by enameled wares and the Yung Chêng and Ch'ien Lung blue and white is often of distinctly poor quality."

As I sit before my box of twelve blue-and-white bottles I am aware that with their varied shapes, widely different designs, and variations of blue color they make a charming display. I have taken care in choosing them that the design painted in blue beneath the glaze shall be well drawn with no fuzziness or lack of definition. I have tried to make sure that the quality of the porcelain should be smooth to the touch and unpitted. The bases have the marks of Yung Chêng

NO. 61. MOLDED PORCELAIN. The design molded in relief and painted. See page 83.

NOS. 62–63. RETICULATED PORCELAIN. This type is made of two bottles in effect, a molded openwork sheath covering a solid bottle forming the base. See page 84.

or Ch'ien Lung upon them, or merely a circle or some small symbol. We have been told not to expect to find the mark of K'ang Hsi. As I have mentioned elsewhere, during his reign an edict was issued prohibiting the K'ang Hsi mark on these perishable objects. Their broken pieces might end on a rubbish pile and the name of the emperor dishonored. So, though we long for a K'ang Hsi piece, the finest of the blue and white, we know we shall not find it so marked. What do I really know about the dating of these bottles anyway? What do any of my collector friends know about dating their blue and whites?

Looking critically at my twelve bottles, much as I like them, I am convinced that there is no K'ang Hsi among them. I have never had a chance to buy one. This conviction may be due to the fact that twice I have looked at blue and white and had it seem to speak to me authoritatively and say, "I am the K'ang Hsi blue and white, the best of this type that was ever made!"

I had that feeling when I looked at a small vase from the J. Pierpont Morgan collection, now owned by Martin Schoen of New York City. I had the feeling again when I looked at No. 57 owned by Arthur Loveless of Seattle. I once had the same feeling when viewing a tray of blue-and-white bottles in the Colonel Blair collection in the Princeton Art Museum. At a recent viewing of these bottles again I was not so sure. It is because of these experiences that I take a sceptical view of my own blue-and-white collection, and that of most of my fellow collectors. Except by the rarest chance a K'ang Hsi blue-and-white snuff bottle does not appear upon the market.

If we find the dating of these porcelain bottles a great uncertainty let us take heart from the comment of Warren E. Cox, a man whose two volume work, *The Book of Pottery and Porcelain,* is well known and who is himself at times a worker in ceramics. Somewhere in the above-mentioned volumes he makes the assertion, "Actually when we get down to facts there is little or no real *proof* that such a vase is K'ang Hsi and such a one Ch'ien Lung or that such a piece is Yung Chêng and such a one Ming. It is not always the easiest thing in the world for a collector to be sure that some odd specimen was made before or after the 450 year stretch from Sung to Yung Chêng days, though this is, of course, easier. We can only go on the rather vague and often badly translated Chinese written descriptions, on the comparatively few drawings which were none too perfect in color or scale and on putting two and two together."

The bottle numbered 54 is of steatitic or so-called "soft paste" porcelain. W. B. Honey says of this that it is almost the only blue-and-white porcelain of fine quality made after the close of K'ang Hsi's reign, apart from archaistic copies of Ming pieces. Père d'Entrecolles says it was made with a special ingredient believed to have been steatite or soapstone and was reserved for small pieces like snuff bottles or other small objects constituting the furniture of the scholar's table. It is described as of a creamy white color with a faint crackle. For a number of years this bottle stood out among my blue and whites as exhibiting most "quality." The enthusiasm of a fellow collector succeeded finally in getting it away from me. Perhaps he was more sure than I that it was a steatitic blue and white. John Pope of the Freer Galleries in Washington, an authority in this field, assures me he was right, however.

Bottle No. 55 is decorated with geometrical designs enclosing conventionalized chrysanthemums. It is a pleasing bottle, good to the touch. For what it is worth it has the Yung Chêng mark on its base. The mark is not well drawn and I have come to feel that a carefully made, highly prized bottle would have a signature that is meticulously inscribed.

Bottle No. 56 has apparently the trees and landscape in continuous design that we frequently find on cylindrical bottles. It is only when you come to look closely that you find every mistaken tree to be a Chinese lion. I have never in any other bottle seen this trick played upon us.

Bottle No. 58 has a landscape design in an underglaze of rust color. We are told that there was difficulty in the firing of this underglaze red or rust color derived from copper. Many times it would come from the kiln with the lines of underglaze design fuzzy and blurred. The results of the firing of underglaze blue were much more dependable. The example shown has a clearly defined design and was one of their successes.

Now come the carved and molded porcelains. No. 59 has the design of the "hundred antiques." The designs appear against an incised background which we call "graviata." This bottle with the design of the "hundred antiques" appears in many collections. It is in the Art Institute of Chicago, in the Fuller collection at the Seattle Art Museum, and I have found it also in private collections. The same theme is often depicted on large porcelain vases.

W. B. Honey says of this decoration, "The Chinese fondness for a vague symbolism is shown in the numerous emblems common on all classes of porcelain. The *po ku* or 'hundred antiques' are of this character. The archaic vase with peacock's feathers is symbolical of the mandarin's rank and a branch of coral signifies longevity; these, with the apparatus of the scholar's table and the musical instruments and the rest, served to recall the antiquarian interests and delights of the cultured Chinese. Here as elsewhere a hundred signifies a multitude rather than a fixed number. The Hundred Deer and the Hundred Boys are further instances."

No. 60 is a carved molded bottle in a lovely combination of grey background and pink-and-green enameled decoration. Against a background of flowers there is a dragon in high relief on one side and the phoenix bird on the other. No. 61 is a finely molded porcelain bottle.

Nos. 62, 63 are what we call "reticulated" bottles. Each is made of two bottles really, a molded, lacey, openwork superimposed upon a solid bottle beneath. Mr. Hitt, in his letter quoted earlier in this chapter, gives a good description of how these bottles were made. It was a difficult technique and the bottles did not wear well. We find many that are nicked and broken. The perfect ones are found so infrequently that they are fairly high priced. The two bottles illustrated have the most common design, the Chinese lions chasing the golden ball. They all have a similar triple border at the top and a single border at the base. They come in all combinations of color.

No. 64, also a "reticulated" bottle, has again a common design, a dragon against an openwork background of leaves. This design also appears in many colors. We have it here in a monochrome yellow. I have often heard collectors say "Such bottles are a great mystery. How this undercutting down to a basic bottle is done is beyond our understanding." I think Mr. Hitt's explanation a most plausible one.

No. 66 is a broad spade-shaped bottle with the painting of three cocks on one flat surface, two on the other. In seal characters the Ch'ien Lung reign mark is

NO. 64. RETICULATED PORCELAIN. The dragon design against a lacy background of leaves is a common motif in this type.

NO. 65. MOLDED BLANC DE CHINE. Again the dragon motif, this time appearing against a wave pattern.

NOS. 66–67. PAINTED PORCELAIN. Two examples, each respectively with the Ch'ien Lung and Chia Ch'ing reign marks carefully drawn on the base. The reign marks are not reliable, but the quality of the workmanship is equal to the best.

carefully drawn on the base. Is it really a bottle made in Ch'ien Lung's time? All we can say is that the bottle is well enough done to warrant our thinking so in this case. Notice the perfect placing of the three cocks. Our eyes are led toward the center of the group, not outside the frame of the picture.

No. 67 has a meticulously painted design of flowers. There is a similar design on each side of the flask-shaped bottle, with enough small differences to show that it was freely drawn. The shoulders and short neck are covered with a conventionalized design of the same flowers. There is a carefully drawn reign mark of Chia Ch'ing on the base, showing that even in the time of this penurious, art-stifling monarch some beautiful work was done.

Collectors who have picked up their bottles only in the best Oriental shops have no realization of the number of wretchedly made snuff bottles that exist, poor enough in shape and color and in design to make you say you hate the sight of a snuff bottle. I have looked over a collection brought back from China by a man who said he had little to spend and whose aesthetic sense unfortunately was as low as his funds. He admits to having paid much less than a dollar each for his hundred or more bottles. You wonder when such bottles were made and for what market. Many of these have a smooched indecipherable reign mark on the base.

This deterioration of the snuff bottle is similar to the decline which took place

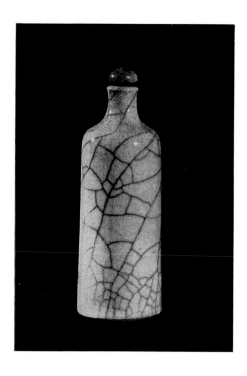

NOS. 68–69. CRACKLED PORCELAIN. Crackle is caused by the uneven contraction of glaze and body when cooling after firing. Its technique so perfected that desired effects could be achieved at will. These two are examples of fine and coarse crackle. They are respectively from the collections of Albert Pyke, Los Angeles, and Harold Sooysmith, Portland, Oregon.

in the Japanese woodblock print. It is inconceivable that from the masterpieces of Kiyonaga, Utamaro, Eishi, and others the print could have sunk so low. The atrocities that were printed after 1850 by Kunisada at his worst and the garish-colored, over-crowded designs that followed his work, run a close parallel to the deterioration we find in the late snuff bottles. Doubtless, too, contemporaneous with the finest of snuff bottle production there were crude utility snuff bottles made. They were all the poorer people could afford.

Though once in a great while we find a porcelain bottle where we feel that the crackle or "crazing" may have been done by time, yet the technique of crackle was so well understood by the porcelain makers that they seem to have been able to produce it in almost any degree. Crackle is caused, so they tell us, by unequal contraction of glaze and body. The former, shrinking, is divided by a mesh of lines which may be further marked by coloring rubbed into them before the piece is cold. Père d'Entrecolles describes the use of "powdered white pebbles," probably pegmatite, to produce a special glaze to create crackle. We learn that the size of the crackle was determined by the number of coatings of this specially prepared glaze. By another account a crackle is said to have been produced by heating the glazed vessels in the sun and suddenly cooling them in water. It is known that the potters were able to determine beforehand the size and shape of the mesh by the appearance of areas of different character in a single piece. These varieties were distinguished by the Chinese by such names as "cracked ice," "crab's claws," "fish roe," "trout-scales," or the "thousand-fold millet." Among snuff bottles we find all degrees of crackle. Nos. 68 and 69 are examples of a fine and a coarse crackle.

CHAPTER EIGHT

The Mysterious Ku Yueh Hsuan

The mystery of Ku Yueh Hsuan reads like a detective story. Lovely milk glass and porcelain snuff bottles and vases have received that name. Translated, it means "Old Moon Pavilion." Who made them? Where did they come from? How did they get their name?

There are many theories about Ku Yueh Hsuan among the writers on Chinese art, but they appear to be in agreement on only one thing—the exceedingly fine quality of this baffling ware.

"Every artistic and technical skill was lavished upon these little gems, which are certainly among the masterpieces, if not THE masterpieces of ceramic art in China."*

"Specimens of Ku Yueh Hsuan are frequently appraised by native connoisseurs as more precious than jade (and this is no figure of speech) and these masterpieces of miniature painting . . . find equal appreciation in the Occident."**

"The finest of Ku Yueh Hsuan pieces are rare, costly and obviously Palace productions. Mr. Yang Hsiao K'u, in his exhaustive study of Ku Yueh Hsuan, lists only 103 pieces known to him of which 50, when he wrote in 1934, were in the Palace collections. There are, he thinks, less than 20 genuine pieces in Europe and America together, and not more than 6 in Japan. . . . According to the Shuo Tz'u they are the finest of all the productions of the Ch'ing (Manchu) dynasty and as their price was astounding many imitations were made which were correspondingly costly."***

Fairly early in my snuff bottle collecting days I had purchased from one of our local dealers a bottle which quickly became one of the favorites of my small collection. I suspect I may have felt myself very extravagant to have stretched to paying him forty dollars for it, but the intrinsic beauty of the piece had made

* Extract from a report of the Smithsonian Institution, Washington, 1902. pp. 346–47.
** B. A. De Vere Bailey, in *Burlington Magazine*, December 1935.
*** Soame Jenyns, *Later Chinese Porcelain*, 1952.

a strong appeal. When a visiting New York collector, going through my bottles, offered me $250 for it my surprise was great that it could command such a price. Beautiful bottles at that time were constantly reaching the West Coast from the Orient. Only the expectation that another bottle of equal quality would soon be showing up led to my decision. I sold my little bottle.

The catalogue card, extracted from my snuff bottle file reads as follows:

> *No. 58*   MILK GLASS
>
> *Exquisite miniature painting of birds and flowers on each side of this bottle. Ch'ien Lung mark in carefully drawn and raised characters in blue enamel on the base. One of my favorite bottles.*
>
> *Source —*
> *Price $40*

A year or so later, on a trip to New York, I was going the rounds of the Oriental shops and as always went into C. T. Loo's to see Frank Caro. After looking through his snuff bottles we sat for a while and discussed collectors and collections. I inquired about a well-known collector who was writing a book on the snuff bottles. "Do you think he has been in the collecting game long enough to be able to write a good book on them?" I asked. I was remembering that he had been a beginner about the same time as myself.

"Yes," answered Mr. Caro, "I have looked over parts of his manuscript and I believe it is going to be a very fine book. It goes slowly because he is a very busy man." Then he added, "Have you seen his wonderful Ku Yueh Hsuan bottle? He got it somewhere out on the West Coast. He won't tell us the source, and he paid only $250 for it. He brought it in for my appraisal soon after he got it. I consider it unquestionably a genuine Ku Yueh Hsuan bottle."

"And at what did you appraise it?" I murmured.

"Anywhere from $1,500 to $2,000," he answered.

The expression on my face and my burst of laughter betrayed me. "The joke is on me, Mr. Caro! I was the one who sold him that bottle!"

"What in the world was the matter with you?" he asked in astonishment.

"I was a fairly inexperienced collector," I answered. "I had purchased the bottle from an experienced Oriental dealer who, like myself, had failed to recognize it for what it was. I paid him forty dollars for that bottle," I laughed.

NOS. 70–72. KU YUEH HSUAN. Three examples from the Seattle Art Museum. Nos. 70 and 72 have the Ku Yueh Hsuan characters on the base, and are close simulations of the real Ku Yueh Hsuan work. No. 71, a genuine Ku Yueh Hsuan, has the Ch'ien Lung mark on its base. See page 99.

"I loved the bottle," I added, "but at the time I was sure others like it would turn up."

"Not in a life time!" Mr. Caro said, shaking his head.

Later in the day I had luncheon with Mr. Martin Schoen whose small collection of snuff bottles is the finest I have ever seen. He was full of the story of the Ku Yueh Hsuan bottle which our collector friend had acquired. "$250 for it! It is worth $2,000!"

I was prepared this time, and I did not in the least betray myself as the former owner of it. "Has Mr. Yau seen the bottle? Has he passed on it as authentic?" I asked. (Mr. C. F. Yau is an authority on Chinese art and I had come to have tremendous respect over the years for his opinion.)

"I would not need Mr. Yau's opinion," he retorted. "I know Ku Yueh Hsuan when I see it. I have two of my own. Not for $250," he put in, "but if I did not have those two I could not rest till I had that bottle! Those Ku Yueh Hsuans are 'the last word' in beauty for a collector of bottles."

I called up my un-named collector friend, the man who had bought my bottle. I asked to see his collection as I always did on my visits to New York.

The story had got around. He knew I had learned that the bottle I had sold him was a Ku Yueh Hsuan.

"I thought you were angry with me!"

"About what?" I innocently inquired.

"About that Ku Yueh Hsuan bottle I got from you."

"Don't be absurd!" I answered. "Collecting is a game, isn't it? Of course I'm not angry. Had the roles been reversed and I had found that your appreciation of it did not extend beyond $250 I would have tried to buy it from *you*. After all, you took a gamble, didn't you? It might so easily have been worth not a cent more than the $250 you paid for it."

"Well, I must say you're a good sport!"

"Collecting *is* a sport," I retorted. "It's a wonderful game we play for the fun there is in it. It's an embellishment of life, but certainly not life itself about which we may very well be serious. To me it is just a wonderful game. If I couldn't take it that way I wouldn't be in it."

This ought to mark the end of my experience with Ku Yueh Hsuan bottles. But strangely it doesn't. There is another story to tell.

We collectors in Los Angeles, I have often felt, have a tremendous advantage over those in any other large city. We all know each other. We get together and pool our knowledge. We are well acquainted with each other's collections. If a visiting collector comes to town there is usually a round of "snuff bottle parties." Such a situation exists nowhere else that I know of. When I visit in New York, Washington, or Chicago, I may know a number of individual collectors but they do not know each other. No event ever gets them together. One New York collector who had been welcomed into our group while visiting in Los Angeles was well aware of the stimulation such gatherings add to collecting. On his return to New York he ran an advertisement in strategic spots to try to form such an informal club. There was not a single response.

Dealers do not introduce one collector to another. I have heard this declared as a general policy. Perhaps they feel that too much trading may go on, that it will divert business, that knowledge of other dealers, auctions, and private sales will be disseminated and again divert business. It is due to the fact that one dealer in Oriental art in Los Angeles, Gertrude Stuart, has thought otherwise that here in this city we snuff bottle collectors are a group. She has taken pains to make us known to each other. In the days when she brought wonderful bottles back from the Orient she would gather us all together for her first showing. That our selecting and buying might be fair and without favoritism there was no private showing, and at our gatherings the procedure was devised of drawing numbers to determine the order in which we should make our choices for bottles. This plan had been my own suggestion.

NOS. 73–75. KU YUEH HSUAN. Three Ku Yueh Hsuan bottles whose authenticity has never been questioned. From the collection o Martin Schoen, New York. See page 99.

Not long ago we were having such a gathering. Many fine bottles were on display. Did my eyes deceive me, or wasn't just such a bottle as I had once lost on the table before me! Another Ku Yueh Hsuan bottle, an exquisite miniature painting of birds and flowers on milk glass, the type of bottle I had once so confidently felt would come my way again! I turned it over in my hand and there on the base in the characteristic raised blue enamel was the reign mark of

Ch'ien Lung. I turned away. Would anyone else recognize it, not for what it was, but just its great intrinsic beauty? The Frontispiece shows the two sides and base of this bottle (No. 1: the base with the reign mark is also shown above).

I stood back and watched. Nothing else interested me. There were ten of us, and I saw the collectors passing it by, perhaps because the price was high. Then my keenest rivals, a husband and wife collecting pair, of impeccable taste, caught sight of it. They looked at it closely, and a glance shot between them told me all I needed to know. It was their choice.

Never had the drawing of numbers which gave us the order of our choosing meant so much to me. I drew number nine! Maybe I turned pale, I don't know. I would be next to the last to choose. I hadn't a chance.

My dejection may have communicated itself to a new collector who sat at the table beside me. Her card was beside mine, number two. "You're way down the line. I'm not playing tonight. I told our hostess I wasn't buying this time. Take *my* card," she suggested innocently. How little she knew that there was anything at stake.

Turmoil inside me. I have never been so aware of the devil sitting on my shoulder as at that moment. With card number two I *did* have a chance. I had but a single choice to fear in that group of ten, my husband-wife collectors, and they had but one choice between them. My hand hovered over the two cards— the nine and the two! But could I ever enjoy that bottle if I got it by such an unsportsmanlike trick? I would not be playing the game, the game whose regulation I had myself suggested.

It is good to remember for the sake of my recovered self-respect that I was sitting back in my chair with card number nine in my hand when first choice was made. It was my husband-wife collectors. They held card number one and my bottle was gone! It would have been gone anyway, even had I yielded to that little devil clawing on my shoulder. But I knew that I hadn't.

Did my sportsmanship prevent me from offering to trade any bottle I had, the best in my collection for that desired bottle? No, I confess it didn't. But there are collectors who are never traders, and the possessors of the bottle I wanted stood firm. With the idea in my mind that I might some day write this book and include the above scene among my adventures, I have waited mischievously to let them learn from this page what I think their bottle really is.

I doubt if I shall ever again own a Ku Yueh Hsuan bottle, but my interest in the mystery of its origin and its "Old Moon Pavilion" name persists. I have pondered many of the theories. It may interest other collectors to know what they are.

Soame Jenyns in *Later Chinese Porcelain* points out a significant fact—that none of the early European writers on Chinese ceramics, Jacquemart, Julien, Du Sartel, Gulland, and Brinkley mention Ku Yueh Hsuan at all, nor does any mention of it occur in the pages of *T'ao Lu* and *T'ao Shuo,* the Chinese sources. He points out that Mr. Yang Hsiao K'u's work is the most authoritative and exhaustive work on the subject. This was privately printed in Peking in 1933 and is difficult to come by. After considerable search for it I shall have to rely on a summary of his findings by B. A. De Vere Bailey, whom I shall quote later.

According to Soame Jenyns one of the earliest references to Ku Yueh Hsuan ware appears as late as 1902 in the work of Mr. Hippisley of the Maritime Customs in a sketch he called *Ceramic Art in China*. He gives the myth of a Mr. Hu, which has been continuously repeated in later writing, even down to 1944 when *The Book of Pottery and Porcelain* by Warren E. Cox was published.

As Mr. Cox tells the story, "At Peking were Imperial glass factories under the supervision of an artist whose name was Hu. As the component parts of the written character Hu, if separated, read Ku Yueh, meaning Ancient Moon, naturally enough Hu adopted the studio name of Ku Yueh Hsuan, meaning Ancient Moon Pavilion. This glass was made in the Yung Chêng as well as the Ch'ien Lung reigns and the Emperor once expressed his admiration for the painting in enamel on it and wished that the same effect could be produced upon porcelain, whereupon T'ang Ying set out to make porcelain that looked like the glass and also did his best to copy the Ku Yueh Hsuan style of decoration consisting of floral designs and landscapes with figures, at times in foreign taste, very delicately painted and with an unusual amount of light and shade while being at the same time in the softest of colors. The glass was translucent and the porcelain gave a semblance of the material in its milky texture and glassy finish."

This then is the Hu story for which the Oriental researcher Yang Hsiao K'u finds no proof.

R. L. Hobson, in the text of Sir Percival David's magnificent catalogue of Chinese pottery and porcelain, published in 1934, gives us a résumé of this and other theories:

"One account makes Ku Yueh Hsuan the art name of one Hu, who distinguished himself as a maker and decorator of glass. The story goes that the Emperor admired some finely enamelled opaque glass of Hu's manufacture and requested T'ang Ying to reproduce its qualities in porcelain. This implies a porcelain with decoration in the style of Hu's glass.

"Another account makes the Ku Yueh Hsuan a pavilion in the Palace precincts in which it is said that some of the choicest porcelains were decorated by specially appointed artists, and the seals attached to the poems which occur on these wares are held to be signatures of these artists.

"A third explanation makes the Ku Yueh Hsuan a pavilion in which the best porcelain of the period (the early eighteenth century) was preserved, and the sponsors of this theory include among Ku Yueh Hsuan wares all those exquisite pieces which are distinguished by a reign mark or hall mark in raised enamel.

NOS. 76–77. IMITATION KU YUEH HSUAN. Painting on milk glass. Each has the Ku Yueh Hsuan mark on the base. I have never found the genuine to have this mark. See page 99.

There is no doubt that the specimens with raised enamel marks are as a rule of very high quality and obviously for Palace use.

"We have no means of judging the relative merits of these three theories. But we can only state them and leave the question for future evidence to decide. But we do recognize certain types that are peculiar to the so-called Ku Yueh Hsuan group. There are several specimens so labelled in the Peking Palace collections and we have seen others elsewhere. Among them are small vases painted with landscapes and figures of shepherds, shepherdesses and sheep in a mannered style with a distinctly European flavour and probably by artists of the school of Castiglione (Lang Shih Ning). Others have exquisite paintings of flowering plants, birds and insects. Common characteristics of these pieces are a peculiar dead white and glassy porcelain which gives support to the theory that the ware is an imitation of opaque glass. Poems are inscribed in the field of decoration usually with red seals appended, one before and one or two after and a period mark (usually that of Ch'ien Lung) in raised enamel on the base."

Western knowledge of Chinese porcelain is based to a very large extent on two important works: the *Ching Tê Chên T'ao Lu,* a detailed report of the porcelain industry at the imperial potteries. It was published in 1815 and translated in part by Stanislas Julien. Also the *T'ao Shuo* written by Chu Yen and published in 1774. This has been fully translated by S. W. Bushell in *Description of Chinese Pottery and Porcelain*. It is significant that in neither work is mention made of Ku Yueh Hsuan ware, nor in a fairly complete record of T'ang Ying's management of the great porcelain works at Ching Tê Chên is there any reference made to his supposed reproduction of Hu's glass.

Mr. Bailey, in his analysis of Yang Hsiao K'u's scholarly treatise says, "A persistent search of available native records was made by him. Yang Hsiao K'u regards the total lack of biographical reference to Hu or his ware as satisfactory evidence in itself that the accepted theory is myth only, and ascribes the evolution of the ware to imperial interest in foreign colors and European designs. Yang believes the Ku Yueh Hsuan story is of latter day commercial weaving. In the period to which they are assigned Ku Yueh Hsuan porcelain under that name did not exist, but pieces of it were merely outstanding examples of ceramic manufacture later to be invested with a ready-made history in the Chinese market place. Note that the finest porcelain examples show only the reign marks or more rarely the dynasty mark which implies no specific origin aside from manufacture under official auspices."

As late as in the winter number of *Oriental Art*, 1949–50, there comes forth a new theory by Sheila Yorke Hardy. She calls her article "Ku Yueh Hsuan, a New Hypothesis." She sticks to the name Hu, even though the existence of that gentleman has been discredited. But Hu also means fox, the character for which, on account of a Chinese superstition, can never be written. Split into its component parts, *ku yueh* however, it would not offend the fox and was thus used to designate the fox chamber in which the high-ranking mandarins kept their seals. Some one of these, an aesthete probably, ordered small objects of art to be made for his fox chamber, and had them marked as such with this circumlocuted name. But in the heavily-laden Chinese script these characters *ku yueh* also mean ancient moon. Hence the name.

This hardly does justice to Miss Hardy's carefully worked out argument. Read her article and see what you think of it. To me it is not convincing.

After many hours spent on this mysterious subject, weighing the opinion of many authorities, perusing many books, there is one conclusion which seems to me most likely: the opinion of the scholarly Oriental who did his researches upon the spot and with no barrier between himself and the written records. He is convincing in his belief that Ku Yueh Hsuan was a name fabricated for commercial purposes a considerable time after the production of the ware. It was applied to the most costly and most beautiful milk glass and porcelain with a certain type of Western design and coloring. On the base of it appeared either the reign mark

NOS. 78–80. IMITATION KU YUEH HSUAN. Excellent specimens with which I try to comfort myself for probably never aga n owning the real thing.

of Yung Chêng or of Ch'ien Lung, but never a Ku Yueh Hsuan mark. When we find the Ku Yueh Hsuan characters it is seldom upon an example of the superlative workmanship to which experts attach the name. This mark was applied to the imitations which came later, after the legend had been started.

It is surprising to find as the only illustration of Ku Yueh Hsuan in Bushell's *Chinese Art* (Volume II, Figure 74) one of these inferior pieces, with the Ku Yueh Hsuan mark admittedly on its base. Collectors are continually finding such late specimens and discarding them eventually as unworthy of a really fine collection.

It seems reasonable to believe that the finest bottles and vases known later by this name were made in blank at the factories of Ching Tê Chên and sent for decoration to Castiglione and other Jesuits who by imperial order had a school of painting in Peking. It would account for the Western influence so discernible in these pieces. Castiglione was known to be a fine painter both in the Occidental and the Oriental manner. Those pieces signed with the Manchu dynasty mark only, and which are considered the earlier pieces, may have been done in the late years of K'ang Hsi's time. I have mentioned elsewhere that there was a period when his name was omitted from perishable pieces. Look out for the bottles signed Ku Yueh Hsuan (古月軒). They are the imitations of which there must have been many.

Speculations have been reviewed as to who made these beautiful things and where. You have been given a carefully sifted opinion. But where the name came from—unless we consider it a mere trade invention—apparently remains as much a mystery as ever.

The imitations of this precious type of bottle vary greatly in quality. Some are so fine that it takes much experience, a sort of developed "sixth sense," to determine them from the genuine.

Twice over a period of years I have stood for a long time before a small case of snuff bottles at the Philadelphia Museum of Art. In that group of fifteen or twenty are as beautiful snuff bottles as I have ever seen in this country in either private or museum collections. Two, in my opinion, would receive a unanimous verdict among experts as being Ku Yueh Hsuan. A number of the others are so close in quality that they sing with the same beauty. What tells you they are not? Certain intangible characteristics are lacking perhaps. If they were before us, in our hands, I might try to tell you, but I am not sure that I could. My confidence in my own opinion rose not long ago when I stood with Miss Emily Tupper, Registrar, in front of the snuff bottle cases at the Seattle Art Museum. I had asked her about Ku Yueh Hsuan bottles, and she took me to the three in the collection that are so listed. They are all three beautiful bottles and are illustrated here (Nos. 70, 71, 72).

"I can take them out of the case for you if you would like to see the marks," she offered kindly.

"Yes, I would," I answered promptly. "But let me tell you what I believe we shall find. That middle bottle will have on the base the mark of Ch'ien Lung in raised blue enamel letters. The ones on either side, that lovely one with flowers around a rock, and the other with two quail will have the Ku Yueh Hsuan mark."

I am sure I was almost as surprised as herself when that was exactly what we found. Miss Tupper admitted it was the middle bottle for which a good deal of money had been paid.

Besides the close imitations of the Ku Yueh Hsuan's loveliness, however, such as Nos. 70 and 72, we have all found quite ordinary bottles with the Ku Yueh Hsuan mark upon their bases. Very often they are as poor as Figure 74 in the second volume of S. W. Bushell's *Chinese Art*.

Nos. 73, 74, and 75 are Ku Yueh Hsuan bottles of whose authenticity there has never been any question. They are from the collection of Martin Schoen of New York City.

Nos. 76–80 are pleasing bottles in my own collection with which I try to comfort myself for probably never again owning the real thing. Every one of them has the Ku Yueh Hsuan mark upon the base.

CHAPTER NINE

Jade & Other Semiprecious-Stone Bottles

Which is your favorite snuff bottle? This is a question collectors often ask each other. If we cannot get an answer we come back with another. Which is your favorite type of bottle? Almost always we find it is jade. Even a visitor who may know little about snuff bottles and the endless variety of materials from which they are made, if asked which type of bottle he would like to see, is almost certain to say, "Your jade ones." He may have heard that it is the favorite stone of China.

Jade has, indeed, been the favorite stone in China. The very name for it, *yu,* means "the gem supreme." Confucius, who lived six centuries before Christ, once said of jade that "in it men find the likeness of all excellent qualities."

Jade appears in two forms, nephrite and jadeite. Nephrite has come from Chinese Turkestan and has been in use for twenty centuries. Jadeite appeared much later, not until Ch'ien Lung's time in 1750, and comes from Burma. This being the case we would be wise to date our jadeite bottles no earlier than the latter half of the eighteenth century.

Nephrite and jadeite are so similar in their appearance, particularly when carved, that they are hard for the novice to distinguish. Nephrite is composed of a silicate of lime and magnesia with a specific gravity of 2.9 and a hardness of 6.5. Jadeite is composed of silicate and alumina, specific gravity 3.2–3.4 and hardness 7. In spite of this difference snuff bottle collectors have difficulty in telling them apart. Polished nephrite has an oily appearance, polished jadeite a vitreous, glassy lustre.

When I think of nephrite I remember a portion of the famous Bishop collection on exhibition at the Metropolitan Museum of Art. They were archaic pieces and of course nephrite. To recall the best of jadeite I remember the lace-like carving of lovely translucent bowls in the Seattle Art Museum. A recognition of the difference between the two is doubtless a matter of experience, though Whitlock and Ehrmann in their *The Story of Jade* suggest a test for specific gravity and describe a means of doing it yourself. Since the book may not be at your elbow I quote their description:

ꓶ "This test for specific gravity is made with the aid of a specially constructed balance in which the pan at one end of the beam is suspended about six inches higher than that at the other end and has, moreover, a hook on its under side. To this hook the jade piece which is to be tested is suspended by a silk thread, which latter has the advantage of a negligible weight in addition to a strength capable of supporting a dead weight of ten ounces. Thus suspended, the jade piece is balanced by weights in the other pan and its weight recorded.

"The jade piece, still suspended as above, is then completely immersed in a vessel filled with cold water and weighed again. Its weight in air (the first weight recorded) divided by the difference between its two weights will give the required specific gravity. The importance of this test becomes apparent when we consider that the specific gravity of jadeite is 3.32, while that of nephrite never exceeds 3.00, a difference well within the limits of careful weighing."

Pure jadeite would be white with no tinge of color. So also nephrite. Colors which exist are due to the admixture of impurities in their composition. Most people think of jade as being either green or white. It is a surprise to many that jade is found in almost every color of the rainbow. We find it in red, pink, black, brown, yellow, grey, all gradations of green, and even blue. Edith Griswold of Stratford, Connecticut, has a blue snuff bottle, definitely blue. It is the only blue jade bottle I have ever seen out of thousands of bottles.

Though we may sometimes buy a jade bottle for the quality of its carving it is usually the color which decides us in the selection of a bottle. If we are looking for a white one we try to get as pure and translucent a white as possible—a jadeite preferably, rather than a nephrite. Grouped in one illustration are jade bottles of apple-green, white, and lavender hues (Nos. 81, 82, 83). The different colors seem to intensify each other. No. 84 is a white jade bottle magnificently carved in the shape of a "Buddha's hand," a certain citrus fruit so called in the Orient because of its finger-like forms.

We all want a fine green jade, the closer to jewel jade the more desirable and the higher in price. A real jewel jade, as I have said before, would not be carved into a snuff bottle; its value in jewelry would be too great. We content ourselves with an "apple green" and consider it fortunate if we find it in a smooth, even color. Sometimes we find brilliant splashes of green on white, "pine branches in snow" the Chinese call it, and this is sure to be jadeite. We find bottles in all shades of green, and it takes great restraint to hold ourselves to one.

If we are seeking a black jade we want it as deeply black as possible. My own, though it has a bit of brown jade upon it which has been carved in relief into an eagle, is as evenly and deeply black a bottle as I have ever found (No. 86).

Nos. 85 and 87 are of less dense black but they both have very fine carving.

We often wait long to find a satisfactory lavender bottle. The lavender is often of faint tint fading into white which sometimes covers a disproportionate amount of the bottle area. A really deep lavender is hard to find. One would hardly expect to get it for less than $150.

Red jade bottles are found in most collections. They are never as brilliant a red as we sometimes find in carnelian but a darker more brownish red. My own red jade bottle is red on one surface only. It fades off into an indeterminate green on the reverse side. A more desirable red jade bottle would be red throughout.

Often there is a yellow "skin" upon a jade bottle, the result of weathering. See Nos. 88 and 89. In such cases the "skin" is not cut away by the lapidary, but cut into a design like an overlay. On one such bottle, a greyish-green jade (No. 90), one flattened side is covered to quite a depth with such a brownish yellow "skin." There, carved in relief, is a woman's figure, a basket of flowers on one side, a crane on the other, the branches of a pine tree over her. Another yellow jade bottle (No. 91) has a deeply cut autumn leaf carved from the brown skin. These bottles sometimes show slight marks of the chiseling where the "skin" has been cut away down to the basic bottle. There are examples of such carving in most collections.

A white jade bottle, carved throughout its surface with a design of grapes, has on its base a small area of this orange "skin." This has been carved into a tiny squirrel, following the traditional theme of "the squirrel and the grapes," which is one of the most common subjects portrayed in Chinese art. I have a jade carving of "a fingering piece" which has the same theme, but in this, as in other pieces I have seen, the artist gives you a hunt to find the squirrel. Wherever you find grapes carved, look for the squirrel. I have searched Will H. Edmunds' *Subjects of Chinese and Japanese Art* for some clue to the meaning of this theme and found nothing. In Katharine M. Ball's *Decorative Motives of Oriental Art*, however, she makes this comment:

"The Chinese say that the reason for combining the squirrel and the grape vine, apart from their equally picturesque possibilities, is that as the vine is able to creep all over and cover everything in its course, so the squirrel, in its perpetual scampering about, can with equal facility cover every available surface within the range of its activities."

If a collector is seeking to get all types he will try to secure a good example of "chicken-bone" jade. It is greyish white, opaque, and full of very fine cracks. Some authorities imply that it is jade which has been through fire, others that its texture is due to long burial. It is a fragile bottle, more brittle than the usual jade. Some in this type are plain, depending on the network of cracks to give it an interesting appearance, others that I have seen are finely carved.

 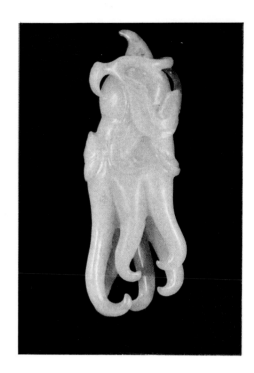

NOS. 81–83. JADE. The range of colors in jade is surprising, including even blue. The different colors of these examples seem to intensify each other. See page 102.

NO. 84. WHITE JADE. A magnificently carved bottle in the shape of a "Buddha's hand" fruit. From the collection of Carl A. Kroch, Chicago. See page 102.

Collectors see many bottles that are called Han jade. The books on jade do not mention it. Han jade, of course, has no reference to the dynasty which existed centuries before snuff bottles were thought of. The name is used to denote burial jade, jade which has been buried with the dead. There has existed a superstition that jade prevented the decay of the human body, hence many pieces were put into the tombs. After such burial, whatever the original color, the stone is said to have taken on the greyish brown colors we find in this tomb jade. This also may be a superstition, although there may be some scientific explanation for the color of these burial jades. The books may not mention Han jade because all this is pure supposition.

So various are the colors of jade that a number of other minerals may be mistaken for it. Soapstone, though resembling it closely, is soft and can be detected by scratching. Aventurine, a variety of quartz, has a green color not unlike jade. Carnelian is sometimes of a color that resembles red jade and is of as great a hardness. Jasper may be mistaken for jade, and Williamsite, a translucent green serpentine, is similar in color to some of the shades of spinach nephrite. Whenever there is doubt a reputable dealer will submit his bottle to the testing of the Gemological Institute.

Jade mining has always been a considerable gamble, for the crude blocks, weighing from a few ounces to nearly a ton, are auctioned off at the source, and until they are cut nobody knows the range of colors that will be found. Jewel jade, the finest of the green jade, bringing its owner a fortune, is always hoped for. Jade dealers, who buy and rough out the stone, farm out the carving, drilling, and polishing to contractors who hire the artisans. Two men cut a block of jade by drawing a wire charged with emery across it. Oftentimes it is a child that keeps the cut supplied with a paste of emery and water.

The methods of the Chinese lapidary have changed little over the centuries. The tools cost but little. They include a small worktable, a lathe which is simply an iron rod supported by a block of wood, a metal disc, and a narrow bench which the craftsman straddles while he works the two treadles to revolve the lathe. His hands are free to hold the object and release abrasives. A diamond drill is worked by hand. Of late years there has been added but one improvement in the polishing, and that is the abrasive, carborundum. It is a handicraft demanding infinite patience. There are no motor-driven tools.

I have watched a Chinese jade carver here in Los Angeles, working with exactly the same equipment as I have described. He told me he found it commercially inexpedient nowadays to carve anything but jade rings. His raw jade material he undoubtedly found right here in this country, for the United States,

NOS. 85–87. BLACK JADES. A uniform black jade is hard to find. Inclusions and variations in color in these three have suggested the designs. Nos. 85 and 87 show fine carving although the black of No. 86 is more intense and even. Nos. 85 and 87 are respectively from the col ections of Georgia Roode, San Juan Bautista, California, and Arthur Loveless, Seattle. See pages 102–3.

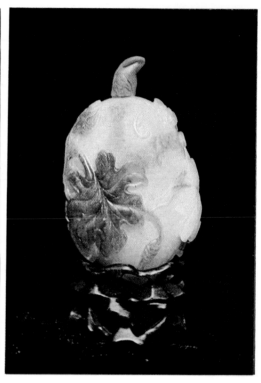

NOS. 88–89. WHITE JADE WITH YELLOW "SKIN." The "sk n" is seldom cut away by the lapidary. From he collection of Edith Griswold Stratford, Connecticut. See page 103.

NOS. 90–91. JADE WITH CARVED "SKIN." Two good specimens of carving of the "skin" in jade bottles. Examples of this type are found in most collections. See page 103.

unlike China, has rich deposits of jade. I spent interesting hours with this Chinese. He knew well the wonderful intricate carving that had been done in the old days by his countrymen. Perhaps he could have done it himself. He had many examples of fine carving, treasures which he showed me with pride. "Too many months of work to do such carving now. No one would ever be willing to pay for it," he said.

Let us now go from jade to other semiprecious stones. Precious and semiprecious are loose terms, however. Jade of the finest quality would certainly rank among the precious stones and its price would reflect it. Ruby, on the other hand, though usually classified as precious, would in its poorer qualities rank only among the semiprecious.

Lest the prices of these semiprecious-stone bottles discourage you I shall not tell you what they are. As I have pointed out in other chapters it is possible to find great pleasure in collecting if one limits oneself to the much less expensive glass or quartz, both of which appear in great variety. Prices placed upon these semiprecious stones are not entirely due to their intrinsic value; they depend upon scarcity quite as much as upon beauty.

Fluorite is a common mineral, sometimes colorless but more frequently exhibiting tints of yellow, green, blue, and red. Pure fluorite contains 48.7 percent of fluorin and 51.3 percent of calcium. It would be used for jewelry and art objects more often if it were not so soft and fragile, for it lends itself to fine carving. The fluorite bottle shown in Chapter II (No. 5) was once illustrated in the magazine *Antiques* (November, 1948), where it was listed as aquamarine. This stone it resembles very much when it is of a bluish hue. The owner of this bottle confidently believed it to be aquamarine. When it eventually came into my possession, I found it could be scratched with crystal, showing it could not be aquamarine. It required a testing at the Gemological Institute to determine it was fluorite.

Tourmalines are alluring bottles on account of their translucency and their lovely color, ranging from pink to deep rose. There is green and yellow tourmaline also, but these colors are less often found in bottles. This stone is composed of a complex aluminumboro silicate with a specific gravity of 3.1 and a hardness of 7. Doubtless because it is found over most of the world it does not rank in the precious-gem class, but its beauty would warrant it. It is said to be found in considerable abundance in California and shipped to the Orient for cutting. No. 4, shown in Chapter II, is a tourmaline.

NO. 92. TURQUOISE. This is a very porous stone and when much handled the original blue tends to turn green, as in this case. See page 109.

NO. 93. SERPENTINE. A yellow bottle. It was sold to me as jade, but I would have known otherwise if I had scratched it. The softness of this stone has limited its use in jewelry and art objects. See page 110.

NO. 94 AQUAMARINE. A beryl stone of the color of sea water. No. 6 shows a carved aquamarine. Here it appears as a plain stone, its beauty dependent upon its color. See page 110.

NO. 95. GREEN BERYL. This differs from the aquamarine only in its color. Its substance is the same. We find it carved and uncarved. From the collection of Elmer Claar, Northfield, Illinois. See page 111.

The opaque, rich, grass-green malachite used for bottles is composed of copper carbonate with a specific gravity of 3.7 to 4, and a hardness of 3.5. Its soft but dense composition has appealed very much to the Chinese lapidary for carving, but there is no suitable malachite in China. It comes to them from Russia. I prefer the uncarved stone on which the shaded rings and mottlings give us enough beauty (No. 3). I have seen many fine carved bottles, however.

I searched long to find a lapis-lazuli bottle to suit me. There lingered in my memory the superlatively lovely ones in the Natural History Museum in Chicago. They are in the Mrs. George T. Smith collection there. I could not accept the dark-navy-blue lapis lazuli which keep appearing because they are as devoid of glamor as the utility blue serge dresses women used to wear. At its best lapis lazuli is a brilliant blue. Though composed of calcite inclusion it is impregnated by three different minerals, all of them silicates of soda and alumina and all blue in color. Its specific gravity is 2.4 and its hardness is 5 to 5.5. I have the pleasurable theory that if you know exactly what you want and wait actively for it long enough, it will finally come your way. No. 2 is a lapis lazuli.

Herbert P. Whitlock, in his *Story of the Gems*, speaks interestingly of turquoise of which many snuff bottles have been made. "There are few gem stones that link together present-day usage with the glamor and romance of the past as does the opaque sky-blue turquoise. Beside the sophisticated jewelry forms in turquoise in the shop windows of Fifth Avenue or Bond Street we can set the marvelous inlaid ornaments made of mosaic-like patterns of turquoise that go back to the time when Egypt was young. In fact, the earliest group of jewelry forms known in the world, the bracelets of Queen Zer of the first Egyptian dynasty, are set with alternate plaques of cast-gold and carved turquoise."

The blue color, which is the only gem qualification of this stone, is due to the copper present in its composition. It is a complex phosphate of aluminium and copper with a specific gravity of 2.84 and a hardness of 6. The fact of its being a porous stone has an influence on its sky-blue color. A bottle which has been much handled is almost certain to have lost its blue color and become distinctly green. My own bottle, which shows considerable crackle, is decidedly green (No. 92). I may at some time acquire a really blue turquoise, but I shall suspect that it has been recently carved or perhaps never handled as a snuff bottle.

NO. 96. TURQUOISE. Elaborately carved bottles like this are called cabinet pieces. They were produced for collections, not for practical use. From the collection of Albert Pyke, Los Angeles. See page 111.

NO. 97. JADE. Another cabinet piece with exceptional carving. See page 111.

Efforts, they tell us, have been made to render turquoise impervious to moisture and grease and thus permanently blue in color, but so far without success. There are, so we are warned, bottles of composition turquoise, made from the powdered stone. These are likely to be of even blueness, perfect, without a trace of matrix or flaw at any point.

Occasionally a snuff bottle made of serpentine comes our way. Unless we think of scratching it to test its hardness we may believe it to be jade. My own yellow serpentine bottle was sold to me as jade, but I would have known otherwise if I had scratched it. Its specific gravity is 2.6, its hardness but 2.5 to 4. It is a hydrous magnesium silicate, widely distributed on the earth's surface. It is doubtless its softness that has kept it from being used more in carving and jewelry, for its color is often attractive (No. 93).

Among snuff bottle collections fine ruby stoppers are occasionally to be found, but like jewel jade if ruby is of jewel quality it would never be carved into a snuff bottle. It is a form of corundum which when a transparent red is classed among the really precious stones. In another color it is sapphire. I once saw a bottle said to be ruby, but it was carved of such unevenly fractured, clouded stone that neither its appearance nor its price were attractive. Just recently, since beginning the writing of this book, another ruby bottle has appeared upon the market. Though far from the brilliant color and transparency of the jewel ruby there is richness and beauty in its even-textured opaqueness and its deep purplish red color. I took it to the Gemological Institute.

"I don't really need to have this tested," I said. "It's a ruby bottle, I'm sure. I am judging from the best of the ruby stoppers that occasionally come our way."

My gemologist took it in his hand. "It's a ruby bottle all right, an amazing bottle, not of jewel quality, of course. But, no ruby of jewel quality has ever been found as large as this bottle. If it were of jewel quality of this size you could, well, you could buy Los Angeles."

"What is the degree of hardness of corundum, where is it on the Mohs scale?" I asked.

"It is very hard, next to the diamond in hardness. In fact, nothing but diamond dust could have cut and hollowed this bottle." He stirred the tiny gold spoon inside the bottle discovering, as I had done before him, that the bottle was deeply hollowed inside.

One of the most beautiful of the stones is the aquamarine and its name, sea water, describes it quite accurately. Most aquamarines range from greenish blue to bluish green and their color is thought to be due to oxides of some of the alkaline earths and iron. It is a beryl gem stone, related to its much wealthier cousin, the emerald. No. 94 is an uncarved aquamarine, while in Chapter II is shown a beautifully carved one (No. 6). We find snuff bottles of green beryl (No. 95). It is said to appear in various shades of yellow, and the name morganite has been given to a beryl of beautiful rose pink color. Somewhere there may exist bottles of golden beryl or of morganite, but I have not yet found them. There may be many other strangers. A collector is always hoping to meet them.

Though the first production of snuff bottles was for utility we know that they soon began to be made as art objects, and at length especially designed for collections. We call such especially designed bottles "cabinet pieces." The finely carved turquoise (No. 96) and the jade bottle (No. 97) would be classified as such. The projections of the carvings would have made them impractical to carry in the sleeve or in the girdle.

CHAPTER TEN

Snuff Bottles of Organic Materials

The list of bottles made of organic materials is a long one, materials which have once been living, growing substances. These would include amber, coral, buffalo horn, rhinoceros horn, ivory, hornbill ivory, jet, mother-of-pearl, tortoise shell, tangerine skin, bamboo, wood, nuts, and lacquer in its various forms. There may be others, but all of these named I have seen used as material for snuff bottles.

Amber is the fossil resin of a species of pine tree that has no living representatives today. It has a specific gravity of 1.5 to 1.1 and a hardness of 2.5. It can be scratched easily, is brittle, and takes on a high polish. The test we use to determine whether a bottle is amber or not is to rub it swiftly back and forth on wool, then see if it will pick up a piece of tissue paper. Glass, with which we may be confusing it, will not pick up paper but amber will.

China's supply of amber has come from Burma, and its color runs from cream yellow to dark red, and from clear to cloudy. It is often beautifully transparent, but some amber bottles are decidedly opaque and uneven in color. These are usually referred to as "root amber." Bottles are carved by the lapidary method, not by edged tools. There is a processed amber for which we should watch out. This when rubbed will not pick up paper. Being comparatively soft the bottles lend themselves to very beautiful carving (No. 108).

Coral bottles are usually expensive, ranging from sixty to a hundred dollars and more. When we know that the coral reefs in many places in the world extend for miles it must be that even-colored and unflawed pieces of coral are found only in small pieces and infrequently. We notice that in coral figures, which are seldom very large, the posture of the figure seems often to be dictated by the irregularities of the original material. The dictionaries give us this information: "Coral is a general term for the hard calcareous skeleton secreted by marine polyps for their support and habitation. Specific gravity 2.6 to 2.7, hardness 3 3/4." We find coral snuff bottles in pink and in red. Nos. 109 and 110

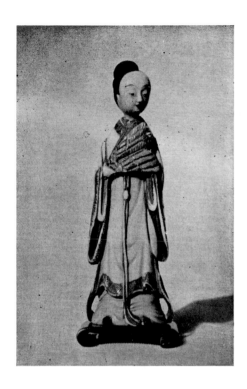

NO. 98. CARVED IVORY. The head forms the stopper. An intriguing bottle to the beginning collector. Later we are affected by the unfair disparagement that it is Japanese.

NOS. 99–100. CARVED IVORY. These types are also considered to be of Japanese make.

NO. 101 (below). CARVED IVORY. The cap serves as stopper. No definite agreement as to whether this is of Chinese or Japanese origin. From the collection of Elmer Claar, Northfield, Illinois.

are coral bottles, one in high relief and one in low relief carving. Occasionally we are offered a rare white coral, but upon having it tested it is usually proven to be something else. White coral does exist, however.

There are rare and finely carved bottles of buffalo horn and rhinoceros horn, but these come our way but seldom. No. 114 is a rare buffalo-horn bottle with bugs of many kinds carved all over it. The hornbill ivory bottles have become important enough in our collectors' game to have deserved a chapter by themselves.

Warren Cox tells us that "aside from the elephant (and its ancient relative the mammoth) the narwhal, the walrus and the hippopotamus, there are no animals which have produced ivory of any real value." Most of the ivory snuff bottles are elephant ivory and furnish some of the most beautiful in our collections. Among the twenty-seven workshops established by Emperor K'ang Hsi in 1680 in Peking there was one for ivory carving, and craftsmen from all over the empire were brought together to produce fine work.

Though many of the ivory bottles are Chinese, the Japanese also seem to have made many of them. Collectors seem to disparage these Japanese-made bottles, perhaps because they were imported for a Chinese usage, or because they have been made recently. Many of them are attractive, nevertheless. The figures of women, with heads that serve as the stoppers are said to be of Japanese origin as well as many of painted ivory. A Pasadena dealer insisted these figures were Chinese because she had bought a considerable number of them in Peking. She probably did, but it is quite likely that they were imported. Nos. 98, 99, 100 we consider to be Japanese ivory bottles.

Recently a collector friend looking over my bottles challenged me on the classification of these ivories. "How do you know which are Chinese and which are Japanese, definitely *know*, I mean?"

He had pricked a bubble! How did I really know? Pondering the reasons that lay back of my classification I decided they were based on nothing more definite than what I had been told at the time of their purchase and on the unsupported comments of other collectors.

NOS. 102–4. CARVED IVORY. Debatable whether Chinese or Japanese. Qua ity of workmanship alone, however, should determine their desirability. No. 103 is from the collection of Russell Mullin, Beverly Hills, and No. 104 from that of Adolph A. Kroch, Laguna Beach, California.

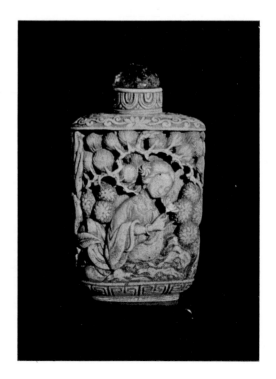

In a search for a better criterion I took my box of fifteen ivory bottles under my arm and went to see Mr. M. Hasegawa, our Japanese friend who for years has done magical repair work for us when accidents happen to our treasures. Not long ago I took him a beautiful porcelain bottle from which half the lip had been broken off. I didn't even have the broken-off piece. When I went to get it a miracle had been performed. No one could ever tell where the break had been. Even an age crackle on the top had been simulated so that it covered the whole. The restored piece must have been modelled and the whole refired. I stood regarding it with amazement. Then I burst out: "Mr. Hasegawa, if you can work wonders like this on a portion of a bottle, why wouldn't it be possible for you to make such porcelain bottles? People pay a lot for them, you know."

I said it half joking. To my surprise he took the bottle back in his hand and seemed to be seriously considering my proposal. At length he shook his head. "The time that would have to go into doing such a thing would be too much," was his answer.

I took my box of ivory bottles to him now because as the repairer of broken

NOS. 105–7. CARVED AND PAINTED IVORY. Collectors will have to decide for themselves whether these are Japanese or Chinese bottles.

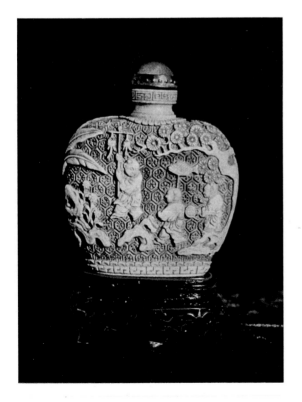

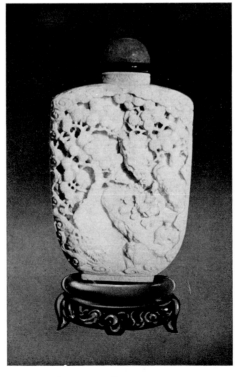

NO. 108. CARVED AMBER. The fossil resin of an extinct pine tree, ranging from cream yellow to dark red. Being soft it lends itself to fine carving. From the collection of Adolph A. Kroch, Laguna Beach, California. See page 113.

NOS. 109–10. CARVED CORAL. Coral bottles range from pale pink to dark red. These are examples of low and high relief carving. See pages 113–14.

art objects he gets to the inside of them, down to the skeleton, as it were. I have known him to come up with astute observations. A broken inside-painted bottle, for instance, had once settled for good and all the question whether those pictures were painted, or whether, as a few collectors had erroneously suggested, they might be what we used to call "transfer pictures." I laid before him my box of fifteen ivories. "Which of these are Chinese, which are Japanese in your opinion?" I asked.

He took his time looking them over. No one ever hurries him. "Why do you think any of them are Japanese?" he inquired. "I believe them to be all Chinese."

I picked up the little lady whose removable head forms the stopper. Everyone has always assured me that this is a Japanese type. "Isn't this Japanese?" I asked.

He shook his head. "A Japanese would have carved a Japanese face. This is a Chinese face. Her garments also are Chinese." One by one on other bottles which I had been assured were Japanese he picked out Chinese features and costumes, even calligraphy not Japanese.

When you get a disturbing diagnosis you go to another doctor. I drove with my box to a long established Oriental shop called Old Cathay. Mr. Z. T. Nyi

NO. 111 (top left). PAINTED IVORY. A desirable bottle, enhancing any collection. From the collection of Virginia Higgins, Arcadia, California.

NO. 112 (top center). CARVED IVORY INLAY. From the collection of Gerry Mack, New York.

NO. 113 (top right). IVORY WITH CINNABAR INSET. From the collection of Russell Mullin, Beverly Hills.

NO. 114 (bottom left). BUFFALO HORN. From the collection of Elmer Claar, Northfield, Illinois. See page 114.

NO. 115–16 (bottom center and right). CARVED WOOD. No. 115 is carved sandalwood originally from the famous Fischer collection made in China. See page 121.

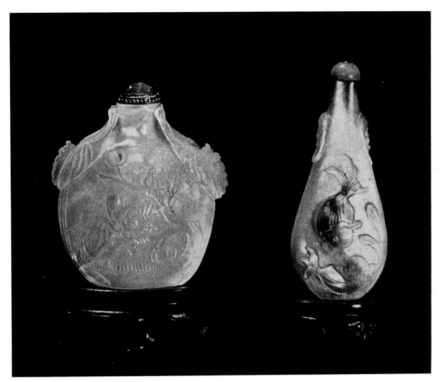

NOS. 117–18. MOTHER-OF-PEARL. Here again the discoloration is utilized in carving the design. See page 121.

NO. 119. WOOD WITH MOTHER-OF-PEARL. Panels of mother-of-pearl on each flat side with *laque burgauté* decoration on the narrow sides. See page 121.

has dealt for a lifetime in Oriental art and has also been to China and Japan many times. I believed he would know. He picked up bottle after bottle saying, "This was made in Japan." In fact among my fifteen bottles he found but three that he could say were Chinese.

When I pointed out the Chinese faces and costumes as Mr. Hasegawa had done he laughed. "Why of course the Japanese artists were carving these for the Chinese trade, and often they were copying Chinese models. But we who have been in the trade for many years know that they were made in Kyoto. But what is the difference? Japanese or Chinese? Why should there be any prejudice among you collectors against Japanese bottles? It is fineness of workmanship that alone should count. If you gave me my choice of any one bottle in this box I would choose this Japanese bottle," he said lifting it out. "It is the most beautiful, the workmanship here is the finest."

I am inclined to believe that his criterion is the true one for us collectors. We should select for fine workmanship and beauty. As to our distinguishing where they were made, we shall have to take the opinion of those who know both Japan

NOS. 120–23. LAQUE BURGAUTÉ. The decoration on a lacquer base is made by the inlay of iridescent shells, often enriched with small pieces of gold foil. One writer has counted as many as five hundred inlays to the square inch. No. 123, below, is from the collection of Gerry Mack, New York. See page 122.

and China, of those who have been on the spot. In general they are in agreement that the figures with removable heads, the carvings of horses and elephants with riders, are the whimsy of the Japanese workshops and that the Chinese tend to let the natural ivory and carving speak for itself without the heavy staining and use of color that seems to designate the Japanese work.

I have dwealt long on ivories because the subject of their origin will always be more or less controversial. Suppose I include Nos. 102–7, and let you collectors make your own decisions.

Jet bottles are made from the same material as was the jewelry fashionable in our great-grandmother's day, and now completely out of fashion. It is composed of a rich black variety of mineral coal, vegetable in origin. It is lighter in weight than the black jade or quartz or obsidian with which we might confuse it.

There are bottles made of wood, and their value depends upon the fineness

NO. 124. TANGERINE SKIN? Who can verify the claim that this is made of tangerine skin processed to become hard and non-porous? It has a leather-like texture.

of the carving. I have a bottle of carved sandalwood which will always remain one of the favorites in my collection. I can remember holding it in my hand one day, part of the George Fischer collection at that time quite inaccessible. I recall thinking to myself that I would give any bottle I possessed to own that treasure. Eventually I got my chance to buy it (No. 115). No. 116 is an interesting carving in another kind of wood. Many different woods were used. We even find bottles carved of bamboo.

There are bottles made of mother-of-pearl. These should be as free of discoloration as possible. No. 117 is quite without flaws. It has a design of bats for handles on the shoulders, and bats clambering up the sides. A second mother-of-pearl bottle has a decided brown area on one side (No. 118). This has been carved into a design of fish, making it more desirable than if the original discoloration had not been there. No. 119 is a wooden bottle with an inlaid panel of carved mother-of-pearl on each side. There is *laque burgauté* decoration on the narrow sides.

I have seen but one tortoise-shell bottle, so I judge they must be somewhat rare. There is a type of agate bottle (I should probably say chalcedony) the markings of which greatly resemble tortoise shell. Collectors refer to it as tortoise-shell agate. This kind of bottle is usually carved very thin, but the genuine tortoise shell would, of course, be much lighter in weight.

There is a curious little bottle in my collection (No. 124) which was sold to me as a bottle made of leather. It has a rough, leather-like texture, but someone who should know has declared it to be made of tangerine skin, processed in some way so it becomes hard and non-porous. This material is said to have been made into other small objects besides snuff bottles. Though my source of information seems reliable I am doubtful about this and invite correspondence from anyone else who can vouch for this. These surely belong among the "novelty" bottles, as do those we find carved out of nuts.

Among bottles made of organic materials there are none in our collections more greatly desired than the lacquer bottles. The Chinese brought their craftsmanship in this material to a high point of skill.

Lacquer is the sap of a tree (the Rhus vernicifera) which is indigenous to China. The tree is tapped when about ten years old. At this stage the sap is a greyish viscous fluid which darkens and hardens rapidly on exposure to the atmosphere. It is collected into large wooden airtight vessels and before use is strained through hempen cloths to remove fragments of bark and other impurities. To rid it of excess water it is stirred in a mild heat, then stored in airtight containers till ready for use.

The use of lacquer in China goes back to legendary times. It was used to cover food utensils and for decoration of carriages, harnesses, bows and arrows, musical instruments, furniture, and many other things. Even houses were decorated with lacquer. When from these larger uses the Chinese turned their skill to the making of small art objects their workmanship was superb. Fortunately the progress made in the art of the lacquerer can be measured beyond the shadow of doubt. Chinese works of art have been preserved since A.D. 756 in the storehouse of the Shosoin at Nara among the treasures of the Japanese emperor of that date. Among the lacquers are a number that are certainly of Chinese origin and furnish the only reliable evidence of the state of the lacquer industry at that early date.*

The Japanese, apt pupils of the Chinese, have in many phases of lacquer work outstripped their masters, yet in the making of cinnabar lacquer carving none have done finer work than the Chinese. They made many cinnabar-lacquer snuff bottles, a name taken from the vermilion color in which it is usually found. The color was derived from cinnabar, red sulphuret of mercury. Layer upon layer of cinnabar lacquer was built up and allowed to harden. The base of lacquer ware is almost always wood, though porcelain and brass and metal alloys are sometimes used. Then the carving is begun with sharp and delicate tools. The cutting, like their brush drawings, must be done without possibility of correction. No. 10, shown in Chapter IV, is a good example of cinnabar lacquer. Sometimes in the building up of the layers a color contrasting with the cinnabar is used. This must be reached unerringly in the cutting of the design.

Imitations have been made of cinnabar carving. The Chinese themselves have in later days cheapened the workmanship by first carving a clay or wooden base and then covering the whole with a single cinnabar-lacquer coating. A strong magnifying glass will usually reveal it, or a slice with a sharp knife in an obscure spot.

Among the most sought after and the most exquisite of the lacquer bottles are those called *laque burgauté* (from *burgau,* meaning shell). The decoration on the black or brown lacquer has been made by the inlay of shells: mother-of-pearl, the nautilus, pearshell and sea-ear.

The iridescent green and blue of the sea-ear has been used, often in combination with tiny squares of gold foil, to obtain charming effects. Each tiny piece of shell and square of gold foil had to be inlaid separately. One of the writers claims to have counted as many as five hundred inlays to the square inch. One of my collector friends, exploring one-fourth of a square inch and multiplying by four declares his count to be as many as eleven hundred to the square inch on a very fine piece. Nos. 120–23 are *laque burgauté* bottles.

Most of these *laque burgauté* bottles have the mark of Ch'ien Lung's reign upon the base. Remembering that among the twenty-seven workshops established by

* Omura Seigai, *Record of the Imperial Treasury, Shosoin,* Tokyo, 1901.

his grandfather, K'ang Hsi, that of the lacquer workers was one of the most flourishing, it is not too difficult to believe that they were made at that time. Encouragement of the arts began to languish soon after that period. It seems unlikely that such difficult and exacting handicraft was done later than in their best period, or that it will ever be done again.

CHAPTER ELEVEN

The Story of the Famous Hornbill

The hornbill-ivory snuff bottle is so rare that many fine collections do not have one. Many of the museum collections can boast no example. The hornbill ivory of which it is made is scarce and therefore expensive. I have yet to know a collector who did not have to part with, at least, three hundred dollars to acquire one. Yes, I do know one collector who found a hornbill bottle in Ireland. The shopkeeper had no knowledge of what he was selling and asked but a few dollars for it. But that was only collector's luck which we all have at times.

The helmeted hornbill from which the material is taken is said to be one of the ugliest of birds. The most extensive story of this bird and the hornbill ivory taken from it is to be found in the *University Museum Bulletin,* Volume 15, Number 4, published by the University Museum, University of Pennsylvania, Philadelphia, an account written by Dr. Schuyler Cammann. This bulletin is still available, and any collector who possesses a hornbill-ivory bottle or hopes someday to have one should have it in his files. Dr. Cammann gives a vivid description of the bird, tells the interesting legend that has grown up about it in Malaya, and describes the way in which the material of the bird's helmet was processed in order to be made into art objects.

The bird measures nearly five feet from tip of beak to end of tail, has coarse reddish-black plumage, with a white stomach and white on its tail. Its two long tail feathers moult alternately, so only one is presentable at a time. There are no feathers at all on most of its neck and back. Since it lives only in the tallest trees it is seldom seen. In China the hornbill ivory taken from it was called *ho-ting,* or "crane's crest." There seem to have been many mistaken ideas as to what animal the material came from. It was sometimes attributed to a crane, sometimes to a fish.

There are said to be some sixty varieties of hornbill birds but only one, the helmeted hornbill possesses the ivory of which snuff bottles, buttons, buckles, thumb rings, and other ornaments for the nobles of the imperial court were carved. This hard substance is found at the front of the head above the beak (the carved skull of this bird is shown here). Its helmet of solid yellow substance is covered at the top and sides, but not in front, by a sheath of brilliant red. It is the gleaming red of this sheath, together with the hardness of the inner substance that has made the helmet so highly prized for carving.

The bird's native home is considerably south of China, and it is not recorded that it was brought into China until the Ming dynasty (1368–1644).

In reading Pearl Buck's *Imperial Woman,* the life of the Empress Dowager, Tzu Hsi, I came with great interest upon the following paragraphs. Tzu Hsi, originally one among the many women of the emperor's harem, had made herself the favorite of the weak-willed emperor of the time.

"They (the nobles of the Court) knew her tricks, and how often the Emperor had been compelled to send her gifts before she would return to him. The last time had been vexatious indeed, for she would not show obedience until he had sent a eunuch to the south, five provinces away, to find some hornbill ivory, that strange substance of the helmeted hornbill which lives only in the jungles of Malaya and Borneo and Sumatra.

"Tzu Hsi had heard of this bird and she craved an ornament made of the yellow ivory of its high beak, covered with a skin of scarlet. This ivory came first to the imperial court as tribute from Borneo centuries ago, and it was so rare that only emperors could wear the ivory in buttons and buckles and thumb rings and its scarlet sheath was used to cover their ceremonial belts. In the dynasty now ruling the princes of the imperial house still loved this ivory so much that no woman was allowed to wear it, wherefore Tzu Hsi longed for it and would have it.

"When the Emperor explained to her with patience that she could not have it, and how the princes would be angry if he yielded to her, she said she would have i: nevertheless, and she withdrew herself for weeks until in despair he yielded, knowing how relentless and unchangeable she was where her will was concerned.

" 'I wish I did not love so troublesome a woman,' he groaned."

For years the possibility of my ever owning a hornbill-ivory snuff bottle was so slight (not only because they were expensive but because they did not appear on the market) that I contented myself with three of the red-sheathed buckles which came my way. Two of them I bought at different times in Oriental shops where their value was known and their price was as much as a fine jade buckle would be. The third, and really the loveliest, I bought at auction in a group of other things for seven dollars. An Oriental dealer beside me was sure it was plastic. He had never heard of the hornbill, even though he was an importer and had made many trips to China for art treasures. Through a trade with one

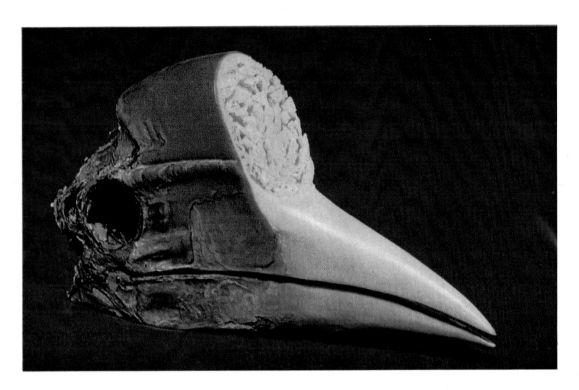

SKULL OF THE HELMETED HORNBILL. A rare bird found in Malaya. It measures almost five feet from beak to tail. Its helmet of solid yellow substance is highly prized for carving into a variety of art objects, including snuff bottles.

of my collector friends I managed to secure a hornbill-ivory *netsuke* and even a skull of the bird's head, more interesting than it is aesthetic. The front surface of the helmet is beautifully carved, as is shown on the skulls depicted in the valuable bulletin on the hornbill which I have previously mentioned. Still a hornbill-ivory snuff bottle eluded me. No. 125 belongs to one of my collector friends and is the finest in color and carving that I have ever seen.

My first chance at a hornbill bottle came when I was offered one with a carved design in the red sheathing on the flat sides of the bottle. This was unusual. The only bottles I had seen had the carved red only on the shoulders, the narrow sides of the flat flask-shaped bottles. This bottle was considerably lower in price than the current price for hornbill and I bought it. On closer study of it I found the body of the bottle to be a fine yellow opaque amber, so near in color to the yellow ivory of the hornbill that it furnished a wonderful simulation of it. The red sheathing had been inserted in the front and back as decoration. The dealer had been very fair. I had been charged only a port on of what a hornbill bottle would bring.

My next hope for a hornbill came when I was calling on an elderly friend in

New York who had a fine collection of snuff bottles. It was a collection made at the beginning of the century, and among them was a fine hornbill.

Every year that I visited New York it had been my habit to call upon him and to enjoy with him his snuff bottles and other beautiful things. Somewhat to my surprise I found that other collectors in New York never went to see him, though they knew of his collection and had seen it once, perhaps. It may have been because nothing was for sale.

On this last visit, which had been arranged through his secretary, I found that the old gentleman had quite lost his mind. He knew me and welcomed me with his old cordiality, but conversation was impossible except in snatches. When he shook his head over a question about one of his bottles and told me that they did not interest him any more, his remark put the idea into my mind that he might let me have some of them. His mental state was such that I felt it might be unfair to deal with him directly about them. He would, I felt sure, be quite incapable of determining fair prices for them. So I talked with his lawyer who had, of course, power of attorney and was managing his estate. He knew my old friend would never look at his bottles again and agreed that I might have those I wanted if I would accept the appraisal of some expert on Oriental art. The appraisal was made on eleven of the choicest. I accepted it, and gave my check for about nine hundred dollars for the eleven.

"When will you be going to the apartment to pick them up?" the lawyer asked.

"Tomorrow afternoon on the way to my train which leaves at four."

"Perhaps it's only fair to get the old man's consent to this. I'll be going to his apartment myself at two thirty tomorrow. Any time after that you can pick them up."

Believing this formality should be a private session between the lawyer and his client I waited in the lobby of the apartment house next day, watching the elevator, watching the clock. The minutes clicked off. I was becoming highly nervous. In a few more minutes I must leave or miss my train on which sleeper reservations had been made.

I was starting to leave when the lawyer and his partner came down in the elevator. He came toward me and handed me back my check. "I know you are going to be badly disappointed about this, but the old man says no, why should he sell his bottles. I have to return your check, but we'll keep track of those eleven bottles you want. We have the list, and I can assure you when my client goes, and it won't be very long now, you will have the very first chance at them. We will see that you get the bottles."

To say that I was disappointed is putting it mildly. Imaginatively I had had those tissue-wrapped jewels, the cream of the collection, inside my purse to pull out and delight in, all the train-trip home. What had gone wrong? How had the lawyer put it up to my friend that he had given a refusal? I had an overwhelming impulse to rush up to the apartment and put the question to him myself. He liked me, he was my friend, he knew my enthusiasm. I was certain he would not have refused me. He would have known, even in his dim state of mind, that his bottles were going where they would be cherished. But there was no time! I would barely make my train.

I rushed to the subway. It was pouring rain. No taxi in those congested streets would have gotten me to the station in time. There was real danger that I would miss my train. I sat on the edge of my seat with eyes bent on my wrist watch, in an anxiety I could not remember experiencing for many years. I rushed into the station with not a minute to spare. Then I suddenly stood still with the jolt of it! All the clocks were an hour earlier than my watch. I had entirely forgotten we were on daylight-saving time!

About a year later, through friends who kept track of things for me I learned of my old friend's death. I sent my check to his lawyer, reminding him of his promise about the Chinese snuff bottles. For some inexplicable reason which I shall never fathom, the answer came back that he remembered no such promise to me. All my old friend's antiques and Oriental art were to be sold at auction at the Parke Bernet Galleries, he informed me. I could come on to the sale and take my chance. I sent a telegram of indignant protest, reminding him of his promise in the apartment lobby with his own partner as witness.

It was one of those things you do to explode your temper. I could hardly have hoped it would do any good. Of course it didn't. But my dander was up. I took a plane to New York to attend that auction. I was going to have that hornbill bottle.

As I studied the catalogue on the plane trip I was deeply disturbed. Among the descriptions and the pictures of the bottles to be sold there was no hornbill listed. Had it been withdrawn and sold separately? Was that the reason the promise to me had not been kept?

When I reached those attractive Parke Bernet Galleries on the morning of my plane's arrival, I made a quick survey of the snuff bottles in their glass cases. Yes, the hornbill was there, but it was grouped with three very ordinary agate bottles, and the four, all described as agate, were to be sold as a lot. On account of the rarity of the hornbill the expert cataloguer for Parke Bernet had failed to recognize it.

I gave hours to the preview, for many beautiful things besides the bottles were on display. I had to hunt for my much-desired eleven bottles and jot down my top price for them in my catalogue. If I don't do this I find I lose my head when the bidding begins.

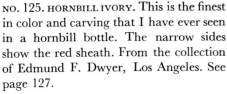

NO. 125. HORNBILL IVORY. This is the finest in color and carving that I have ever seen in a hornbill bottle. The narrow sides show the red sheath. From the collection of Edmund F. Dwyer, Los Angeles. See page 127.

NO. 126 a, b. HORNBILL IVORY. Another example showing how the red sheathing of the hornbill helmet was used by the artisans.

Two incidents at the preview amused me. I stood beside the glass case where the hornbill and the three accompanying agates were exhibited. A snuff bottle collector joined me, a man as aware of the uncatalogued hornbill as was I, for I knew he had one of his own in his collection. We were discussing the preview in general when mischievously I put in, "These agates are extremely ordinary, aren't they? I wonder how they came to be in this collection." "Yes, they are, aren't they?" he answered. He was probably sure that I was missing the hidden hornbill. I tried the same comment on a dealer a little later, and laughed inwardly at his same silence on the hornbill. We are wily folk, we collectors! And the game, if you treat it as a game, is certainly fun.

At the auction the agate bottles, sold in groups of three or four, went consistently for an average of fifteen or twenty dollars each. It must have astonished the auctioneer when one particular group of four went soaring, with a jump of twenty-five dollars at each bid. I put an estimate of ten dollars each on the three agates I would want to get rid of, and pushed my bid for the lot from three hundred dollars to three hundred and thirty. The bottle fell to me!

It is a fine example of hornbill, a flat-sided, squarish bottle, well carved on the yellow sides with figures and trees in low relief. On the narrow sides, the shoulders, is the red sheathing carved in dragons (No. 126).

When I walked into C. T. Loo's Oriental shop the next day Mr. Caro met me with smiles. "Through the whispering gallery I have heard that you got the finest of the snuff bottles at the sale yesterday. It is too much to expect, I suppose, that you would have them with you."

"I certainly do have them with me." I laughed. I laid the eleven choice ones out on the table.

"You did well," he said, "these are fine bottles, the kind that seldom show up on the market nowadays." He touched the hornbill. "Do you want to double your money on the hornbill?" he asked.

To my look of surprise he answered, "Yes, I have a customer who would pay you six hundred for it. He has plenty of money and he wants a hornbill. It is lucky for you that there was no listing of the hornbill in the Parke Bernet catalogue. If there had been you would have had competition over the country."

"No," I said, picking up the bottle and fondling it in my hand, "the pursuit of this bottle has been too long and too arduous. I've got to enjoy it now for a little while."

CHAPTER TWELVE

The Inside-Painted Bottles

Of all Chinese snuff bottles the inside-painted ones are the most astounding. On the inside of these little bottles, seldom more than two inches high, through a tiny opening at the top no more than a quarter of an inch wide, Chinese artists have painted with consummate skill landscapes, portraits, birds and flowers, scenes from their legends, a wide variety of subjects. The portraits are excellent, showing fine modeling of features. These paintings are miracles of genius and craftsmanship, and it is doubtful if they will be done again.

For a long time it was thought that these bottles were done in Ch'ien Lung's time. Even as late as 1953 they are so attributed in a catalogue of a famous collection of snuff bottles exhibited at the China Institute in America in New York City. Mattoon M. Curtis, in his *Book of Snuff and Snuff Boxes,* published in 1935, states that the best of these inside-painted bottles were made in Ch'ien Lung's day. Mr. Henry Hitt whose *Old Chinese Snuff Bottles* came out in 1945 made the same mistake. Dr. Berthold Laufer had come a little nearer the mark. When he wrote the catalogue of Mrs. George T. Smith's collection, now in the Chicago Natural History Museum, he dated the two inside-painted bottles 1835 and 1838.

Perhaps the first grave doubt thrown into this early dating came when Mr. Hitt received a letter from Mr. N. C. Shen of the Department of Psychology, Yenching University, Peking, in 1948. Somehow this Chinese collector of inside-painted bottles had come upon Mr. Hitt's book. He wrote to correct Mr. Hitt's error in the dating of them. It was a letter which shattered the idea of all this early dating. Mr. Hitt realized the letter's importance and generously typed it in many copies to send to his collector friends. For a long time I had a carbon of Mr. Shen's letter in my files, but when we loan such things they have a way of not coming back to us. As I remember it this collector definitely places the making of these bottles in the last quarter of the nineteenth century and the first of the twentieth.

I do, however find a carbon of Mr. Hitt's reply to Mr. Shen which he also sent to me:

Dear Mr. Shen:

The receipt of your letter about painted-inside snuff bottles is a very important event in our research. It confirms and ties together conclusions I had arrived at from many scattered sources. I appreciate it immensely.

The statement in my book (p. 31) that painting inside is said to have originated with Wo Tao-tzu of the T'ang Dynasty is from p. 95 of "The Story of Snuff and Snuff Boxes" by Mattoon M. Curtis, a most unreliable source on Chinese snuff bottles. The book Pi-yen Ts'ung-ko, containing four essays on snuff bottles, published in 1870, does not, I am told, have any reference to painted-inside

NOS. 127–28 (above & below). INSIDE-PAINTED BOTTLES. Through an aperture hardly a quarter of an inch wide these paintings were made on the inside of the bottle. These two are by Chou Lo Yuan, the earliest known artist in this genre. See page 136.

NOS. 129–30. INSIDE-PAINTED BOTTLES. These have the signature of Yeh Chung San. There are so many bottles with this signature, however, that we must assume that they are the work of a group. No. 130 is from the collection of Martin Schoen, New York. See page 137.

NO. 131 a, b. INSIDE-PAINTED BOTTLE. One of the best specimens signed Yeh Chung San. The detail is enlarged to about $2^1/_2$ times the original size. See next page.

bottles, though I have not as yet a full translation of it. Bibliotheca Nicotiana, an 1880 catalog of the collection of Wm. Bragge of Sheffield, England, lists 628 bottles, none painted inside. The first published article on Chinese snuff bottles by Marcus B. Huish, in The Studio, London, June 1896, shows a Chou Lo Yuan bottle 1889, the earliest I have recorded. The older museum collections in this country show very few painted inside bottles though modern collections have many. . . .

In addition to stating the corroborating evidence which Mr. Hitt had already found in his own researches as to the late dating of these bottles this letter to Mr. Shen continues with a discussion of the work of the various artists with many questions about them which I have no doubt Mr. Shen eventually answered.

The last doubts in regard to the period when the inside-painted bottles were produced have been removed by the researches of Dr. Schuyler Cammann of the University of Pennsylvania, who has published his findings in *Oriental Art,* Volume III, Number 3, Autumn 1957, and in other publications as well. He not only gives proof that the technique necessary to the production of these bottles could not have been developed before the last quarter of the nineteenth century, but shows that the subject matter of the paintings themselves gives evidence of their dating. His study of collections of inside-painted bottles, notably of the ex-

NOS. 132–35. INSIDE-PAINTED BOTTLES. Representative works by the most popular of these artists, Ma Shao Hsuan. No. 135, below, shows a typical design, sometimes called "the contents of the waste basket." This is from the collection of Gerry Mack, New York. See page 138.

tensive Wolferz and the Mack collections, has settled the matter of the cyclical dating. His work is undoubtedly definitive in regard to these bottles. The articles he has written are a "must" for collectors, and we have the promise of a book by him on this subject in the near future. We now know that this extraordinary art began with Chou Lo Yuan, the founder of the school. His earliest painted bottle so far has been found to be one dated 1887. The school lasted only some sixty years, ending in the late forties with work so crude that collectors do not care to have it in their collections.

No. 127, with a group of animals on each side of the bottle, is by Chou Lo Yuan, the artist whose work is thought to be the earliest, as is No. 128 with a fine landscape design.

While a picture was being taken of No. 131, an inside-painted bottle by Yeh Chung San, I had a section of the painting enlarged. I could not believe that under magnification the painting would not show crudities that would destroy its beauty. Observe the enlargement along with the pictured bottle and marvel, as I do, at the perfection of line, even though it has been magnified considerably.

I had another detail enlargement made of the portrait of a general. The enlargement of the face shows the same skilled definition. Lest the paintings be scratched most collectors remove the spoons from their inside-painted bottles.

No. 129 has the same signature, Yeh Chung San. The work of this artist is found more frequently than any other in our collections. It is impossible that any one man could have produced the great number of bottles which we find signed with his name. It is known, however, that his son, also an inside-painting artist, used his father's signature. Other painters must have done so as well. We have to consider the signature that of a school, I believe. The workmanship varies. We have to view it with a discriminating eye. There are many fine bottles signed Yeh Chung San, however.

The inscription appearing on No. 130 describes the subject of the painting, an historic episode often used by Chinese artists. It is the meeting of Li Ching, who later became one of China's foremost generals, and the famous beauty, Chang Chu Cheng. They are being introduced by General Yang Shu. It is the beginning of a romance. Historical scenes and legends are often the subject matter of these bottles. Sometimes the inscription is a poem. It adds greatly to the

NO. 136. INSIDE-PAINTED BOTTLE. By Ma Shao Hsien, a painter in quite a different style from Ma Shao Hsuan. See page 139.

NO. 137. INSIDE-PAINTED BOTTLE. By Ying Chiu. Works by this artist are not very common, but the quality of the workmanship in this one is good. See page 139.

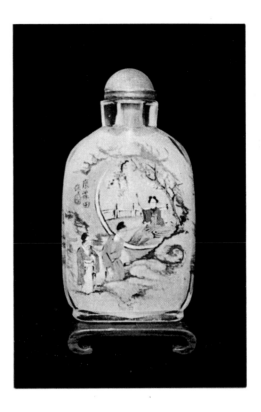

NO. 138. INSIDE-PAINTED BOTTLE. Another popular subject by Ma Shao Hsuan, "the two Ming princesses."

NO. 139. INSIDE-PAINTED BOTTLE. Signed Chang Pao Tien. It is the only inside painted bottle signed by this artist that I have seen.

NO. 140. INSIDE-PAINTED BOTTLE. Another example by Ma Shao Hsien. Most of his works are bird-and-flower designs.

interest of a collection if, like the owner of this bottle, we have the calligraphy translated and kept with the information on our catalogue cards.

One of the most accomplished among the artists of these bottles was Ma Shao Hsuan. In calligraphy and in portraiture he seems to have excelled all the others. One subject that has seemed typical of him and that he has many times repeated has been called "the contents of the scrap basket." In appearance it looks like torn and sometimes partly burned papers thrown upon a table, exhibiting different kinds of calligraphy (No. 135). Though Ma Shao Hsuan repeated the same subjects over and over he nevertheless had a wide range. He did classical landscapes, figures, singly and in groups, portraits, insects, birds, and animals.

The "two Ming princesses," seems to have been a popular design of Ma Shao Hsuan's. It is in the British Museum collection and in a number of private collections with which I am acquainted. On my own similar bottle the signature and seal are on the reverse side from the figures (No. 138). In the illustrations I have seen of the British Museum's bottle Ma Shao Hsuan's signature is on the same side as the beautiful women. In different ways all the bottles vary slightly. They are never an exact copy of one another.

The portrait bottles all collectors find attractive (Nos. 132, 133, 134). The reverse sides have the calligraphy for which Ma Shao Hsuan was equally famous.

Nos. 136 and 140 are by Ma Shao Hsien, no relative of Ma Shao Hsuan's we are told, and a painter in quite a different style. Most of his bottles that I have seen have been of birds and flowers, as are these two.

No. 139 is by Chang Pao Tien, No. 137 by Ying Chiu, both artists whose work we find less frequently.

Occasionally there are bottles which are unsigned though the painting may be excellent. That is true of the next three pictured here. No. 141 is a landscape on blue tinted glass, No. 142, travelers on a mountain road, and No. 143, children playing around a tree.

My enthusiasm for these inside-painted bottles has been so great that there is the disproportionate number of thirty-eight of them in a collection of 350 into which I have tried to gather all the various types. Among these thirty-eight there are paintings on glass, both clear and tinted, on rock crystal, smoky crystal, hair crystal, agate, and amber. On some of the crystal bottles the inside-painted picture seems not enough. They "gild the lily" by carving the outside of the bottle as well.

NOS. 141–43. INSIDE-PAINTED BOTTLES. Three examples of excellent quality, but unsigned. No. 141, painted on a blue-tinted glass, is equal to some of the best works.

Whenever a collector is showing his bottles to someone who is unacquainted with them these inside-painted bottles always seem the most astounding, and as people have sometimes told me, the most memorable.

To make it convenient for collectors to tell by what artist their bottles were painted I add here the signatures of a few of the most important men.

馬 MA	馬 MA	周 CHOU	丁 TING	葉 YEH	孟 MENG
少 SHAO	紹 SHAO	樂 LO	二 ERH	仲 CHUNG	子 TZU
宣 HSUAN	先 HSIEN	元 YUAN	仲 CHUNG	三 SAN	受 SHOU

CHAPTER THIRTEEN

Miscellaneous Types of Bottles

Through this chapter will parade the different kinds of bottles which have not taken their bow in any of the previous chapters. They are a numerous group, and one can never be sure that one has included all of them. New materials are continually turning up.

The metal bottles have as yet had no introduction. Being practically indestructible they may well be as venerable as any we have. I have never doubted the age of my brass bottle, a dated one, with "Shun Chih, third year" (1646) deeply incised upon its base (No. 7). These brass bottles differ in shape and decoration, but the date is always there. Mine has concave sides, similar in shape to the snuff saucers. These concave sides might very well have served the purpose of saucers. The dates on these brass bottles, ranging as they do through the 1640's and 1650's correspond to the time when snuff and the bottles were coming into use. They were for practical use evidently, with good sturdy stoppers to keep the snuff well corked. No. 8, also shown in Chapter III, is a multiple brass bottle, the only one I have ever seen of its kind. Besides the main bottle there are eight small bottles attached, fully equipped with their own spoon and stopper.

I have seen gold snuff bottles. For a number of years there were three in the possession of a Pasadena dealer. I used often to look at them. I would be browsing at the time to find some attractive overlay glass bottle for fifteen or twenty dollars. The gold bottles were quite out of any beginner's range. Some four or five hundred dollars I believe was asked for them. At last they were gone. I have often wondered in whose collection they found a home.

Silver snuff bottles are met with frequently. Most collectors who try to get all types have them. No two are ever alike. They vary greatly in their decoration. No. 144 is a silver bottle. No. 145 is a horn bottle with a mantle of silver decoration.

We do not often see pewter snuff bottles. My own pewter bottle (No. 146) is one of the first I ever owned and no other has since come my way. Like the brass

and the bronze they must have made a good practical bottle for the Oriental to carry in his sleeve. We come to have a special respect for a bottle which is usable. An iron bottle with an inset of silver was shown earlier (No. 9).

Slate, which we also call ink-stone, is a common material. I have owned several and passed them on as some new specimen of finer carving made its appearance. We all want an example of soapstone, but we fail to give this well-carved bottle the respect it deserves because it is so often a cheat. It looks so like jade. We take a look at the price and think we are getting some wonderful bargain. The scratch of a knife soon tells us the truth, however, for soapstone is soft. We are inclined to be prejudiced against the deceiver, but if the carving is fine enough we take it anyway.

The Japanese must at times have made snuff bottles for export to China. In an English publication not long ago an article on snuff bottles made the state-

NO. 144. SILVER. Silver bottles are frequently found. Their designs vary greatly. See previous page.

NO. 145. HORN WITH SILVER MANTLE. From the collection of Russell Mullin, Beverly Hills. See previous page.

NO. 146. PEWTER. Like the brass a utility bottle. Pewter bottles, however, are seldom found. See previous page.

NO. 147. GOLD LACQUER. The creation of a Japanese artisan; they surpassed the Chinese in this type of work. From the Fischer collection made in China.

NO. 148. SATSUMA WARE. Another unusual Japanese bottle, perhaps made for export. Also from the Fischer collection.

NO. 149. EMBELLISHED BOTTLE. Basic bottle of malachite with jade, coral, and pearl insets. A unique bottle. See next page.

ment that no gold lacquer one had ever been found. I happen to have a fine gold lacquer one, No. 147, obviously of Japanese workmanship, and certainly a snuff container. I sent a picture of it to Kyoto where lacquerers still carry on as they have continued to do ever since the finest lacquer was made. I made inquiries about the bottle. The answer came that there was no record in their shops of the making of snuff bottles. This isolated bottle, obviously of their workmanship, must have been a special order issued many years ago. It was originally from the Fischer collection made long ago in China.

I have made no inquiries about No. 148, a Satsuma bottle in my collection. Its shape, small aperture, and top indicate its purpose as a snuff bottle, but the ware is Japanese. It also came from the Fischer collection. Often, as we hold a bottle in our hands we wish for some magic power that would let us know its history. What Arabian Nights' tales these bottles might unfold for us!

Embellished bottles come in all materials. Bits of semiprecious stone, ivory, silver, and gold are used to build up pictures or designs upon a basic bottle. These tiny pieces are inserted very much as a dentist inlays a tooth, and we seldom find a piece missing. I have seen this embellishment on variously colored jade bottles, on colored glass, on milk glass, on agate, and on brown or black

NOS. 150–53. EMBELLISHED BOTTLES. Embellishments of various semiprecious stones upon white jade bottles. No. 153 is from the collection of Harold Sooysmith, Portland, Oregon.

lacquered bottles, even on *laque burgauté*. They are expensive bottles. Much patience and skill have gone into the making of them.

One of the most interesting of my own embellished bottles is No. 149. It has the jade carving of a magnolia blossom inlaid upon malachite. Beneath the blossom is a white jade butterfly with a coral body, and on its wings are two seed pearls and dots of green jade beads. The reverse side has a design of the same theme, with a different arrangement of the flower and butterfly. The three white jade bottles, Nos. 150, 151, and 152, have the more usual type of embellishment. No. 159 is a moss agate bottle with insets of mother-of-pearl forming the decoration of bird and flowers. No. 160 has the same type of bird-and-flower arrangement in mother-of-pearl set in a blue opaque glass which beautifully contrasts with it. No. 161 is a fine green jade bottle with tiny figures set in various materials.

With apologies to the miscellaneous bottles which I may have failed to include here, let me finish with an important group that we call the enamel bottles. Enameling was a Western art. French artisans who came to China during the Manchu dynasty were responsible for its importation. It was used in three ways, as cloisonné, champlevé, and as painted enamels. The Chinese called these painted enamels "foreign porcelain." So acceptable to the Chinese was

NOS. 154–58. ENAMEL. A group of enamel bottles. No. 154, with an unusual *mille fleur* design, is from the Martin Schoen collection. No. 155 is from the Seattle Art Museum. No. 156, showing a Western "mother-and-child" painting, is from the Russell Mullin collection. No. 158 has a gilded bronze base and is from the collection of Arthur Loveless. European motifs are common in enamel designs. See page 147.

NOS. 159–61. EMBELLISHED BOTTLES. Three examples of embellished bottles. No. 159 is a moss agate bot le with mother-of-pearl designs from the collection of Edmund F. Dwyer, Los Angeles. No. 160, mother-of-pearl on blue opaque glass, is from the collection of Arthur Loveless, Seattle. The last is a green jade bottle with semiprecious stones and is from the collection of Georgia Roode, San Juan Bautista, California. See page 144.

NO. 162 (below). CLOISONNÉ. Strips of metal soldered at right angles to the base were formed into cells called cloisons. These were filled with enamel powder and fired.

this French innovation that among the Peking workshops established by K'ang Hsi's order was one for the processes of enameling.

In the making of cloisonné the outline of every detail of the design is made with narrow bands or ribbons of metal, soldered edgewise to the base in such a way as to cover the surface with shallow cells called cloisons. These are then filled with powdered enamel of the desired colors, moistened and tightly packed into their cells. They are fired in the open courtyard, protected by a cover of iron network. Men stand by to regulate the fire with large fans. This process has to be repeated several times on account of the shrinkage under heat of the enamel and the pitting which also takes place. Later the surface is ground down to an even texture and polished with charcoal. The metal surfaces of the cloisons are gilded as well as the parts of the surface not adorned with enamel. No. 162 shows a cloisonné bottle.

In the champlevé technique cloisons are not used, the hollows to be filled with color are cut out of the metal with graving tools. Otherwise the process is similar. There are examples in which both methods are used on the same piece.

The painted enamels of China are identical in technique with the painted enamels of Europe. The palette of colors used is the same as with enameled porcelain. The body of the enameled snuff bottle is usually made of copper. Over this copper base a ground of opaque enamel is laid, and on this the colors are superimposed and fired. Owing to the soft nature of the ground these colors sink in, are incorporated with it, producing a loss of brilliance. Very often the designs upon these bottles are European figures. But Chinese figures are used as well. No. 156 is an enameled bottle showing a European mother and child. No. 157 is enamel on porcelain, with European figures on each side. No. 155 is another enamel showing the bust of a European woman. No. 154 is a beautiful enamel with an unusual *mille fleur* design. No. 158 on a gilded bronze base has an oval insert of the enamel painting of a European woman. It is fine miniature painting. I envy the owner of this bottle. The base has, besides the Ch'ien Lung mark, "painted by order of the emperor."

The most beautiful enamel bottles I have seen are in the Colonel Blair collection at the Princeton Art Museum. A few years ago I arranged in advance to see this collection and took the hour's train ride from New York City to do so.

From my record of that visit in 1956 I find the following paragraph:

"7th tray. This was the drawer which took my breath away! It contained eleven of the loveliest enamels I have ever seen. Most of them had the European type of face and decoration. They were of the finest miniature painting. Much of this Blair collection I could have passed over rapidly. Why are collections such a mingling of the worst and the best? I should have saved more time for these eleven enamels. I was thrilled beyond words at the beauty of such superb bottles. No, I found plenty of words, too! Because of my enthusiasm the curator turned to a catalogue. There she read that $5,000 had been paid for five of them. I was not surprised. Though we find Ku Yueh Hsuan in milk glass and porcelain only, there was Ku Yueh Hsuan quality there. Castiglione must have had something to do with them."

CHAPTER FOURTEEN

What Becomes of Our Collections?

If you are a collector there probably isn't a thought in your mind at the present time in regard to your collection beyond the immediate enjoyment of it. Any question about its final disposition has not occurred to you. That's because you are young or in the prime of life. There comes a time, however, when your collection has grown richer and you have grown older, when you begin to ponder its final disposition.

You have doubtless been aware for a long time that your children care nothing for your treasures. If you asked them to look them over with you they might be dutiful, but bored. You know, of course, that except in some very unusual case—and I have known but one—children are not interested in their parents' hobbies. Don't be disturbed by a fact so universal.

If you leave your collections to them, however, a strange thing may happen, and this I really *have* seen. Possession makes all the difference in the world! They become interested because these things are now their own. They begin to think it is time that they found out something about them. I watched this happen in the case of a famous Japanese-print collection. Until the collection became his own possession I doubt if the son had ever given his father's prints more than a passing glance. Now he found himself the owner of something that had brought his father a certain renown and certainly a host of friends. At the time I made the son's acquaintance his interest and his knowledge were so great it was hard for me to believe he had not been the original collector.

So take a chance on your children. You won't be around to know what happens, but if you were it might surprise you.

The worst that can happen is that your children will dispose of your collection. And is that so bad? I think not. The individual pieces will be going into the hands of people who love them and who will enjoy them. That surely is something you would wish.

Please put out of your mind the thought of leaving them to a museum. Museums are not for small things. Let *netsuke, inro,* sword guards, and snuff bottles circulate out in the wide world where they can be enjoyed and handled. Don't sentence them to life imprisonment in a museum where their appeal can be to the eye alone and that through an encasing glass. A tactile enjoyment of these small works of art is as necessary as a visual one. We hardly make the acquaintance of a *netsuke,* an *inro,* or a *tsuba* unless we hold it in our hands.

The museums do not really want them. Most of the museums in the large cities have collections of Chinese snuff bottles which have been left them, but I can think of few where they are properly and permanently displayed. This is true though the amount of cabinet space needed would be only a few feet and need extend but three inches from the wall.

The Seattle Art Museum is one of the few where snuff bottles are well displayed, and you can be sure of always finding them. Perhaps their unusual treatment is due to the fact that the Fullers, the founders of the museum, themselves collected them.

The Museum of Natural History in New York City, perhaps an unusual place to find snuff bottles at all, has been until recently another exception. Here the Drummond collection has been permanently on display. But try to see the several collections of snuff bottles which have been left to the Metropolitan Museum of Art! Every year that I go to New York City I write to the Curator of Oriental Art to ask if I may see the museum's snuff bottle collections. After a number of such requests and each time a frustrating reply, my letters have now grown facetious. I refer to my previous vain attempts and express the hope that this time the bottles may not still be in storage or that the room where they are usually kept is not being redecorated. I get the same courteous letter back, but there is some new reason why I may not see them.

If you are not already aware of the fact, let me assure you that if you ever want to see some specific thing not on permanent display in a museum you must write ahead and warn them of your approach. If you just walk in unheralded and make your request you may be met with a refusal. If you are a determined person, with a temper which you can turn on efficaciously at times, you may accomplish your purpose. You will be made aware, however, that you have disrupted the inner workings of this public institution. Of course it is true that in order for you to see a collection not on display you will be taking the time of a museum attendant which would otherwise be given to these inner workings. At the moment you may be inclined to stress the prime purpose of a museum and be unsympathetic about the priority of what goes on behind the scenes. Be just, however, museums are doubtless understaffed. But be wary, too. Let them know you are coming.

Well in advance of my arrival I wrote the Chicago Natural History Museum asking to see the Mrs. George T. Smith collection of snuff bottles. It took two hours of an attendant's time for me to go through it. I was taken to a storeroom or workroom where the bottles were kept in a big cabinet. A very few of the best ones were on display in the rooms upstairs. Drawer after drawer was brought to a table nearby for my inspection. Here, as so often before, I wondered why collections are so mixed. The badly chosen, crudely carved bottles cheapen and destroy the effect of the whole. It must have pained Dr. Berthold Laufer to have had to include in his descriptive catalogue of this collection in 1913 so many poor bottles along with the fine ones. They should have been culled.

At this point one of my collector friends differs strongly with me. "You are forgetting that people's tastes differ. The bottles you so despise in this collection Mrs. Smith must have thought fine or they would not have been there." My reply to that is that museums should have powers of discrimination when they receive gifts. Their curators are people of trained aesthetic taste. There are, after all, certain criteria on which most of us agree. Poor carving is poor carving wherever we find it. Do museums have to accept *in toto* collections which are given them? My belief is that they would rather not accept snuff bottles at all.

Years before I had come to this same museum, then called the Field Museum, to see Dr. Gunsaulus's famous collection of Japanese sword guards. I was surprised when Helen Gunsaulus, his daughter, then curator of Japanese prints at the Art Institute of Chicago, advised me to take a flashlight along. I learned why. The sword guards were on the bottom shelves of a case so badly lighted that even with the flashlight and down on my knees I did not feel that I was really seeing the guards. This condition may now have been changed. I have never tried to see them again. How much more pleasure there would be to sit down with a collector of sword guards at a table and handle and discuss his treasures with him.

The Blair collection of snuff bottles is at the Princeton Art Museum. If you write ahead and make your arrangements you are well taken care of. The janitor brings up from the basement regions the drawers in which the bottles lie. An attendant courteously gives you two hours or more of her time while you view a collection which holds many treasures. Who at Princeton knows of their existence, and how often, I wonder, are they brought out of their deep seclusion? I wish that I had asked. Who even among collectors knows of their existence? It would be unfair not to mention that there were a dozen or more in a glass case in one of the museum rooms, but the specimens exhibited, at least at the time I saw them, would never tempt one to be a collector. Had the finest of that collection been shown, there would have been beauty enough to catch the eye of any chance museum visitor. But why expect this careful selection? I tell you, the museums do not want them. Snuff bottles are the unwanted little step-children, thrust upon them, unsought.

Over the years, with each new change of dynasty at our Los Angeles County Museum, I have asked to see the collection of snuff bottles given by the Allen Balches. The Balches were people of wealth. In their lifetime they had given the Atheneum to the California Institute of Technology and Balch Hall to my own college, Cornell University. The Balches had traveled widely, they had good taste, their collection of snuff bottles ought to be, for all these reasons, worth seeing. Now that I, too, had fallen for the snuff bottles I was very desirous of seeing that collection again. I would, I knew, look at it with new eyes now that I was a collector myself. Over the years, as I have said, I made numerous requests to see the bottles, but without avail. At length becoming vocal in my exasperation, I roused the interest of a man who had personal acquaintance with the museum people. "I'll get you a chance to see those snuff bottles," was his comment. He did. We were taken down to a storeroom where articles in need of repair, broken porcelains that might be mended, lined the shelves. There on the floor, loose in paper cartons, lay the snuff bottles. Some of the tops were missing from the bottles, a condition impossible in their owner's day. I can't say I really saw the collection. I was too disturbed.

Many years ago a collection of about five hundred *netsuke* was given the De Young Museum in San Francisco. In order to make sure that they would be properly displayed the owner had two cabinets constructed so that the *netsuke* would stand in tiers and be easily seen through the glass. These cabinets are in one of the storerooms. It is years since they have been rolled out into any of the display rooms. There are many *netsuke* collectors in San Francisco. It is a city more Oriental-art minded than any city in the country, thanks, perhaps, to the early days of Gumps. Why is this *netsuke* collection never featured in the museum displays? How is it possible that even the ardent *netsuke* collectors in the city do not know of its existence? I recently met a Palo Alto collector who is writing a book on *netsuke* who had never heard of this collection, doubtless a treasure trove for research.

It is because museums care nothing for these miniature arts. They are not for small things.

Necessary as museums are as the conservators of the arts of the past and exhibitors of the arts of the present, have we not sometimes had the feeling in regard to their treasures that I found expressed by Agnes Meyer in her delightful autobiography, *Out of These Roots*. She had been a close friend and associate of Freer in the forming of his great collection. When the official opening of the Freer Galleries took place in Washington in May 1923 she had this to say:

"Mr. John E. Lodge (head of the museum) and I examined the final arrangements together. All of these familiar objects which I had enjoyed so often in the informal setting of Mr. Freer's Detroit home or in the New York apartments where he lived during his last years of illness, suddenly took on a curious remoteness as if the artificial museum atmosphere had thrown a veil between us that it was difficult to pierce. I said farewell to these beloved treasures as I had said farewell to the friend who had gathered them together just before his death. It is essential to have museums for the products of bygone ages, if only to protect and preserve them for posterity. But the feeling of intimacy with these records of man's spiritual striving is scarcely possible when they are imprisoned in cold and formal settings for which they were never intended."

How much more true is this of such small intimate objects of art as the snuff bottles, the *inro,* the sword guards, and the *netsuke.* And since the housing of such treasures by private collectors presents no problem I make a plea that they be left out of museums and kept in the hands of those who love them, where they can be reached and touched.

Edmund de Goncourt, the great French collector, has expressed my own feeling about the disposal of collections. In his will de Goncourt said:

"It is my wish that my drawings, my prints, my curios, my books, in a word, those things of art which have been the joy of my life shall not be consigned to the cold tomb of a museum and subjected to the indifferent glance of the careless passer-by; but I require that they shall be dispersed under the hammer of the auctioneer, so that the pleasure which the acquiring of each one of them has given me shall be given again in each case to some inheritor of my own taste."

BIBLIOGRAPHY

Bailey, B. A. De Vere, article in *Burlington Magazine*, December, 1935

Ball, Katharine M., *Decorative Motives of Oriental Art*, New York, 1927

Burton and Hobson, *Handbook of Marks on Pottery and Porcelain*, New York, 1928

Bredon, Juliet, *Peking*, Shanghai, 1922

Buck, Pearl, *Imperial Woman*, New York, 1956

Bushell, S. W., *Chinese Art*, Victoria and Albert Museum, London, 1924

——, *Description of Chinese Pottery and Porcelain*, London, 1910

——, *Oriental Ceramic Art*, New York, 1897

Cammann, Schuyler, "Account of Hornbill Ivory," *University Museum Bulletin*, Vol. 15, No. 4, Philadelphia, 1950

——, "Chinese 'Eglomise' Snuff Bottles," *Oriental Art*, Vol. III, No. 3, Autumn, 1957

Cox, Warren E., *The Book of Pottery and Porcelain*, New York, 1944

Curtis, Mattoon M., *The Book of Snuff and Snuff Boxes*, New York, 1935

Edmunds, Will H., *Subjects of Chinese and Japanese Art*, London, 1934

Fenollosa, Ernest F., *Epochs of Chinese and Japanese Art*, Boston, 1912

Gemological Institute of America, mimeographed lectures, Los Angeles

Gilliard, E. Thomas, *Living Birds of the World*, New York, 1958

Goodrich, L. Carrington, *A Short History of the Chinese People*, New York, 1951

Grantham, A. E., *Hills of Blue*, London, 1927

——, *Story of a Manchu Monarch*, London, 1934

Hansford, S. Howard, *Chinese Jade Carving*, London, 1950

Hardy, Sheila Yorke, "Ku Yueh Hsuan: A New Hypothesis," *Oriental Art*, Winter, 1949-50

Hitt, Henry C., *Old Chinese Snuff Bottles*, Bremerton, 1945 (privately printed, o.p.); also unpublished correspondence with collectors

Hobson, R. L., *Catalogue of Chinese Pottery and Porcelain in the Collection of Sir Percival David*, London, 1934

——, *Handbook of the Pottery and Porcelain of the Far East in the Department*, British Museum, London, 1948

Hobson, Siren, Strange, Kelley, Kuntz, and Tomita, *The Romance of Chinese Art*, New York, 1929

Honey, W. B., *Guide to the Later Procelain*, Victoria and Albert Museum, London, 1927

Huggins, Mabel Irene, "Snuff Bottle Garden," *Nature Magazine*, August-September, 1954

Huish, Marcus B., *Chinese Snuff Bottles of Stone, Porcelain and Glass*, London, 1894 (privately printed)

Jenyns, Soame, *Later Chinese Porcelain: The Ch'ing Dynasty*, New York, 1952

Kraus, E. H., and C. B. Slawson, *Gems and Gem Material*, New York, 1948

Lee, James Zee, Min, *Chinese Potpourri*, Shanghai, 1946

MacSwiggan, Amelia E., ' Hornbill Ivory," *Spinning Wheel,* July, 1957
Meyer, Agnes E., *Out of These Roots,* Boston, 1953
Morgan, Harry T., *Chinese Symbols and Superstit ons,* Los Angeles, 1942
Nourse, Mary, *A Short History of the Chinese,* New York, 1943
Omura, Seigai, *Record of the Imperial Treasury, Shosoin,* Tokyo, 1901
Shaffer, Ellen, "Chinese Snuff Bottles," *Antiques Journal,* May-June, 1954
Shipley, Robert M., *Dictionary of Gems and Gemology,* Los Angeles, 1956
Sowerby, Arthur de Carle, *Nature in Chinese Art,* New York, 1940
Volker, T., *The Animal in Far Eastern Art,* 1950
Wentworth, Ann, "Chinese Snuff Bottles," *Antiques,* November, 1942 and November, 1948
Whitlock, Herbert P., *Story of the Gems,* New York, 1936
——, and Martin L. Ehrmann, *The Story of Jade,* New York, 1949
Winkworth, W.W., "Chinese Snuff Bottles," *Country Life Annual,* London, 1954

INDEX

The italic numbers indicate references to plate captions